Defending Human Dignity

Catholic Answers to Gender, Abortion, and Relativism

Informal essays on everything from freedom of speech and religion to gender ideology, sex, and abortion.

Marie Brousseau, B.Sc.Bio, B.Ed.

En Route Books and Media, LLC
Saint Louis, MO

✸ENROUTE
Make the time

En Route Books and Media, LLC
5705 Rhodes Avenue
St. Louis, MO 63109

Cover credit: Sebastian Mahfood
Copyright © 2025 Marie Brousseau

ISBN-13: 979-8-88870-425-7
Library of Congress Control Number: 2025946925

No part of this book may be reproduced, stored in a 'trieval system, or transmitted in any form, or by any means, 'ronic, mechanical, photocopying, or otherwise, without the prior written permission of the author.

Table of Contents

Introduction 1

Chapter One: On Homosexuality and Transgenderism 17

Chapter Two: On How We Got to Where we Are 41

Chapter Three: On the First Proponents of Transgenderism 51

Chapter Four: On Abortion.. 61

Chapter Five: On Freedom of Expression and the Heroes Fighting for Authentic Democracy... 75

Chapter Six: On Truth, Faith and Reason 91

Chapter Seven: On Science 101

Chapter Eight: On Feminism, Education, Marriage and Family. 121

Chapter Nine: On Catholicism and Freedom of Religion 139

Chapter Ten: On Arts and Artists... 151

Chapter Eleven: On Euthanasia and Assisted Suicide and On Death and Suffering... 159

Conclusion... 171

Introduction

I can hear the lamenting cry of the mourning dove coming through the air vent in the ceiling. It's probably perched on the duct jutting out of the roof. What is it decrying today? Another day with its ups and downs? Don't we all have them?

<u>Another day, another controversy</u>

4:37am

I wake up before dawn breaks. The birds are already singing outside in anticipation of the sun rising; I suppose they have a sixth sense alerting them to the first rays of our luminous celestial body working its way above the horizon. I've heard someone, somewhere, expound on the birds' reason for filling the air with their concerted harmonies; they would be raising their voices in glory to God, first thing in the morning! What a beautiful thought. God's creation chanting the service of morning prayers at daybreak. Waking up to an intonation of lauds by an avian choir each morning fills me with wonder.

5:00am

I get out of bed. Six hours of sleep will have to suffice for today. I'd much rather get up, go downstairs and work on my computer than try to stay asleep.

I am a high school teacher. Nowadays, the computer reigns in the classroom. All of my courses are technologically prepared. Another day of braving hordes of teenagers interested in only one thing: their cell phones. It's like an extension of their hands, the way they're attached to them. Why the government didn't ban phones outright from entering school property is beyond comprehension. At long last, this year, in my province, phones are banned from the classroom, albeit not from the school. At least it's a start. I am a product of the generation when cell phones didn't even exist!! Somehow, we all survived the '80s and '90s without lugging around a third appendage. When I cross the main corridor of the school at lunchtime, I see dozens of youth sitting next to each other on the bleachers, each texting their friend instead of engaging in a face-to-face conversation. How can they learn social skills?

The worst part is social media! This is about all they follow: Tik-Tok here, Instagram there, Facebook in between, a dash of X added as seasoning, a lot of YouTube thrown into the mix, and, of course, the never-ending online video games that comprise at least half their waking hours. My perseverance in teaching adolescents is a testament to my commitment to our common future; these students are our next doctors and lawyers, nurses and teachers, plumbers and electricians and, hopefully, mothers and fathers.

But, then again, maybe not. A sizable portion of our students nowadays are sexually active, taking contraceptives and advocating abortion rights. Nobody wants to get married anymore, let alone raise a family. They all want to have sex, with no strings attached. I have heard fifteen-year-old students affirm, in the classroom, for all to hear, that they will do what they want, when they want and with whom they want (I am omitting the vulgar obscenities with which they expressed themselves). It is not uncommon to hear snippets of conversations between female students, explaining to others their use of an intrauterine device (IUD). At least some of the students using contraception didn't want to go as far as abortion, according to what I could hear from my desk eight feet away, while others were quite vocal about their own rights trumping those of the child within the womb. This was in Religion class no less, in response to the Catholic Church's moral doctrine concerning sexuality. Most students in Catholic schools are baptized Catholics, who, for the most part, ignore Catholic teaching and doctrine (for example, some of them do not know what the Eucharist is, saying that they had eaten the funny tasting bread, only once, at their first communion, but nobody told them what it was and they haven't had it since).

This entire contraception mentality has pervaded young minds for the past six decades. Recreational sex versus procreative sex. Women's lib. Equality. Freedom. My body, my choice. Free love. The whole nine yards. Try expressing your traditional views on love, sex, marriage and babies nowadays, and watch the reactions your position ignites on the opposing side. No respectful debate, no freedom of expression, no "I disagree with your views but I respect your right to express them". According to one pro-choice teacher in New York, the pro-lifers, who were merely preparing pro-life signs, were the ones "inciting violence" against the pro-choicers. The teacher in question hurled invectives at the protesting pro-life students and destroyed their pro-life signs, demonstrating her desire that they not express their opinions on abortion.[1] The fact that this educator was relieved of her duties by the college gives me hope that some institutions still believe in upholding the First Amendment in the United States Constitution,[2] which guarantees freedom of expression.

Even though I'm Canadian, I follow closely what happens in America, since Canada is an ally, as well as a follower of all things American. Generally speaking, most of our heads of state here in Canada deliver the same rhetoric as many of our southern neighbours of defending a woman's "right to choose". Choose what? Killing a defenseless child? Right up to the moment of birth? Without limits? Across the board? Mind-boggling! Oops! Excuse me, I forgot: it's not acceptable to use the word "kill"; it's much too negative and violent sounding, not to mention judgmental, for describing an action that is, after all, legal!! I think the popular euphemism of the moment is "exercising one's reproductive health care choice". This sanitized version of "killing" is much more palatable. No feeling of guilt is involved when one is exercising one's health care choice. Why can't people just call a spade a spade?

---

[1] National Catholic Register, Joe Bukuras/CNA/Education, May 23, 2023 (ncregister.com), (https://www.ncregister.com/cna/new-york-professor-vandalizes-student-pro-life-display-and-chases-journalist-with-machete)

[2] whitehouse.gov (The First Amendment provides that Congress make no law respecting an establishment of religion or prohibiting its free exercise. It protects freedom of speech, the press, assembly, and the right to petition the Government for a redress of grievances).

Introduction

My students are naturally interested in all matters controversial. For example, they unanimously chose the subject of abortion for debate class. Of course, they were all on the pro-choice side, so I opted to be a "student" at the event to show them the protocol of presenting one's position and the art of debating. And, yes, I chose to represent the pro-life side. Fatal mistake on my part. It wasn't long before I got called to the administration office to give an account of my actions. It took forty-five minutes of my time to justify myself.

Apparently, the pupils should have been prepared weeks in advance, with the help of psychologists to guide the entire event. Did these students have a psychologist explain to them the ins and outs of sexual matters and the emotional and psychological effects of being sexually active, with all possible consequences, when they decided to embark on their sexual forays? I think not. From what I have heard over the years, most girls whose mothers do not want their daughters to become pregnant are given the go-ahead for the contraceptive pill. I've heard many stories of mothers saying "here", while dropping the circular contraceptive pill box in their daughter's hand as soon as the girl started looking at boys. The girl's response was a smiling "thanks mom". That is all! This is nothing new. When I was in high school, back in the eighties, a bunch of us would listen to other girls boasting about their mom or dad wanting to be informed when they decided to have sex with their boyfriend in order to go to the doctor and obtain a prescription for the pill. The nubile females would then smile at us, with a self-satisfied expression on their faces, while the rest of us looked on, without saying a word.

As I was saying, the subject of abortion was chosen by my students for the debate, which is understandable, given that the very themes of some of the books they are given to read in class deal with sexual matters, in one form or another. Furthermore, these are the same teenagers who are already sexually active and using contraception. If they are deemed old enough to be having sex and using contraception, are they not old enough to be informed about exactly what abortion is?

As for the topic of abortion itself, regardless of the students' current sexual behavior, I did not have the presence of mind to voice the following in my defense: if the subject is so taboo, then it must mean that there is something wrong that needs to be hidden, otherwise, why be so hush-hush about it if it were such a good thing? The pro-choice side is therefore implicitly admitting that there is indeed something wrong about abortion. Why not let the students find out absolutely everything there is to know about abortion (just like any other subject) and let them make their own decision about the rightness or wrongness of it?

Anyway, will I be without a job soon? How far will this go? All because I afforded my students, and myself, the right to express our opinions freely, in the context of a public forum such as a debate. I wonder if I would have had this pushback if I had advocated the pro-choice side? If not, what total hypocrisy. I probably would have been commended on my teaching technique. All it takes is for the pro-choice side to kick up a fuss, thus causing problems for the pro-life side. Of course, after this hullabaloo, it goes without saying that I

Introduction

will not be accepting this topic choice (or any other "hot-button" issue) in the future for the debate unit. We'll have to content ourselves with discussing such topics as which animal makes a better pet: a cat or a dog? Or is this also too controversial? Will I have to defend myself against cat lovers/dog lovers everywhere?

Another controversy which will undoubtedly rear its ugly head to torment me at some future point is the Transgender Movement that is being spearheaded in our schools. This movement has been aggressively pursued in the past few years (around the time that the COVID pandemic cohorts in schools ended). I survived the past thirty-six months in Education basically by cowardice, avoidance and retreat strategies.

Yes, I admit it. I did not have the courage to stand my ground and refuse to cave to the edict of using preferred pronouns. I feel so very ashamed of myself for letting my fear of reprisals and unwanted publicity influence my decision to comply with the mandate of not "misgendering" transgender students and colleagues. I actually addressed some of my biologically female peers as "mister" and used masculine pronouns for my poor overwhelmed female students struggling with this issue. Doing so went against my core beliefs; I felt compelled to do so by the school's mandate and by fears of losing my job.

Fear of the possibility of being arrested (as were some devoted, informed parents in Canada) loomed large before me, and I capitulated. Having to live with one's own lack of courage is quite humiliating, let me assure you. At one point, I had to sit through a two-hour presentation of a transgender educator informing us, the "ignorant teachers", of the correct terminology to use when speaking to/about transgender persons. Included in the oral presentation were the definitions of the endless different genders and self-identifications that anyone can adopt on any given day, as well as what our reaction should be when we make the "mistake" of misgendering someone and how to react when being called out on said mistake.

It's hard to believe, let alone understand, the school board's decision to include such a presentation at school, during a professional pedagogical formation. Shouldn't teachers receive formations on improving teaching techniques and on addressing students' working habits? Or workshops on math, science and literacy courses? I was sitting in the midst of seventy other teachers, listening to their murmurs of assent at each pronouncement of the orator. Everyone around me seemed to be in full agreement with this presentation. Then, to add to this already unusual display, we were all told how we were expected to act going forward. Within weeks, I was called out by a colleague for labeling a female student as "she". I had unknowingly "misgendered" the youth and was peremptorily told to address the student as "he", with an actual index finger pointed at me. I was so taken aback, I literally retreated a few feet, in shock, at the vehemence of the upbraiding. Even the sweet child looked ill at ease and told me not to worry about it, that she didn't mind and had not decided yet which gender she wanted to be. I deduced from this tidbit that the adults were the ones enforcing the gendering mandate in the school, not the students.

I did venture, two or three times, to address this issue with the higher echelon, only to be cut off each time by the administration, being told that "we won't talk about this", or "they are confused and searching for their identity/trying to find themselves", effectively shutting me up. I quickly realized that I had absolutely no allies in this particular school and was surrounded by sycophants who were kowtowing to the prevailing mentality of our culture regarding everything associated with the LGBTQ2SI+/Transgender agenda. And, by the way, this is a (so-called) Catholic school that "proudly" displays the rainbow flag side by side with the huge crucifix in their lobby, along with a second rainbow flag flying high on the staff on their front lawn (going against the diocese's request not to do this).

I later opted for the easy way out and left the school at the end of the year, refusing their offer of a guaranteed position for the new school year. I went elsewhere the following autumn. What did I find there? A bit of the same, though not quite as bold and in-your-face. As far as I can see, the entire school system is more or less following the transgender agenda as well as the contraception/abortion mentality that is ruining society as a whole. Our (so-called) Catholic school board uses our Lord and Savior's very own words of "love one another" as their motto to justify their affirmation and promotion of all the LGBTQ+ issues (not to mention the other false "realities" of our society, such as abortion). They naturally always omit the rest of Jesus's words in His exhortation of loving one another:

"..as I have loved you" (John 13:34-35). We are supposed to love each other as Christ loved us: in truth. He did say *"I am the way, the truth and the life"* (John 14:6), hence that is how we must love each other. Not by agreeing with lies, but by proclaiming, lovingly, the truth. Perverting scripture to justify aberrations is common in many spheres of society, including many politicians who will cite chapter and verse of the bible and somehow use the biblical citations to give grounds for such actions as "transgender care" and "reproductive health care" (aka abortion). One only needs to have listened to such eminent persons as the 46th U.S. President Joe Biden and former U.S. Speaker of the House Nancy Pelosi, both self-described devout, practicing Catholics, making links between their faith and their unashamed support and push for abortion and transgender "rights". And, of course, Canada's previous Catholic Prime Minister, Justin Trudeau, had always been right up there, spouting the same narrative. President Biden had even gone so far as to make the sign of the cross at a pro-abortion rally in Florida, in April 2024,[3] for which he was criticized, given the Church's unequivocal stance on abortion.

All of these agendas, by the way, are being entrenched in schools, without parental knowledge; children can be as transgender as they want at school and parents have no clue. I have seen this phenomenon with my own eyes. This is going on right now in elementary and secondary schools all over the country. School authorities do not have to inform parents/legal guardians of such a momentous event in the child's life. We, the teachers, were all told to not disclose a

---

[3] https://www.foxnews.com/politics/biden-makes-sign-of-the-cross-during-pro-abortion-speech-in-florida

student's "preferred pronoun" to parents, lest they suffer abuse at home because of their decision to self-identify/self-define. We were told to address the students by their biological pronouns when communicating with parents, but to address them by their chosen names and pronouns in the school environment (this smacks of multiple personality syndrome, not to mention blatant hypocrisy and lying by omission). Another warning we received collectively, during a personnel meeting, was to accept male students using female bathrooms, and vice-versa, without question. We were bluntly told that if we had a problem with this, we needed to undergo formations in order to correct our wrong thinking. We were supposedly the ones who were putting up obstacles to inclusivity, and we were told that it would not be tolerated.

Just to put some of this in context, back in 2023, there had been a Bill up for debate in California that would have enshrined into law the mandate for parents to affirm their child's gender choice under penalty of being charged with child abuse: *Under California's Assembly Bill 957 ... a parent could lose custody for not 'affirming' or agreeing to a child's claim about gender identity... This bill makes law that failure to affirm your child's identity is child abuse.*"[4] If something like this can happen to parents, imagine what can be done to anyone else who is responsible for children (i.e. teachers). Fortunately, "*California Gov. Gavin Newsom vetoed a state measure*

---

[4] californiaglobe.com June 17, 2023 (https://californiaglobe.com/articles/under-new-california-bill-parents-would-be-charged-with-child-abuse-for-not-affirming-transgenderism/)

on Friday (Sept. 29th, 2023) that would have required parents to 'affirm gender transitions' for their children or risk losing custody."*⁵* This being said, in July 2024, Gov. Newsom signed a Bill into law *"banning schools from implementing policies that require parents be notified if their child requests to be identified as a different gender."*[6] This particular mandate was the last straw for billionaire Elon Musk, who pulled out his companies (i.e., SpaceX) from California, in protest of the rigid anti-parental rights that Gov. Newsom is implementing.[7] It is to be hoped that, eventually, mothers and fathers will have their parental rights reinstated in order to raise their children without impediments.

The same mindset of hiding essential information from parents is already in place for prescription medications; apparently, from what I've learned, in some provinces in Canada, a child as young as fourteen years of age can contact a doctor for any prescription he/she wants to have, without parental knowledge and/or parental consent. This can be done with the help of school authorities, who tell the child that their parents need not know. I have actually seen this happen and was quite surprised. When I ventured to ask a question, I was told that legally, this could indeed be done.

---

[5] https://www.dailysignal.com/2023/09/25/newsom-vetoes-bill-requiring-california-parents-affirm-kids-gender-transitions

[6] https://www.dailysignal.com/2024/07/18/california-bans-policies-requiring-parents-be-notified-of-childs-pronoun-changes

[7] https://www.ndtv.com/world-news/elon-musk-to-move-companies-out-of-california-over-transgender-law-6121784

I find myself having to constantly weigh my words and not ruffle any feathers, if I want to lead a quiet life without being labeled a bigot, a homophobe, a transphobe, a hate-speech advocate, or any other negative and false slur meant to bully me into silence. And, in addition to bearing this in the workplace, I have to live with this enforced silence within my very own extended family circle. As soon as I start to say something that doesn't mesh with their way of thinking, be it religion, abortion, sexuality or homosexuality, I am met with a barrage of either loud dissenting arguments (being shouted down) or smirking ridicule ("you don't really believe that, do you?" is one common question I get asked, accompanied by a pitying, smiling face). I have since taken the decision to try to be completely silent at family gatherings and content myself with presenting a smiling demeanor. Actually being able to accomplish this feat of the will is another matter.

Don't get me wrong; I love people. Yes, there are gay persons in my familial entourage, in my workplace and in my friendships, and I love them all. I will accept, for example, an invitation to a gay person's birthday party, no problem. However, I will not accept an invitation to a gay wedding, for the simple reason that, however much I may like or love the gay person, I cannot be a part of an action that goes against what I sincerely believe to be the objective truth about what marriage is, and had always been, since the dawn of man. This belief is rooted in my firmly-held religious convictions. Contrary to what most people think, it is possible to love someone without loving what they do, say or represent: love the sinner, not the sin. (Oops! I did it again. I used an unpopular word: "sin". More fodder for the politically correct language police. I wish George Carlin were still with us. He would have had a field day with this whole euphemistic and inclusive language garbage that is being shoved down our throats every day).

Here's another thing I've noticed: the "live and let live" catchphrase of yore is long gone. What is being forced upon society today is "affirm the way I live, or else I will brand you a bigot and a hater". This is pure intimidation tactics and discrimination in reverse. Why do they want our approval and affirmation so much anyway? Is it to justify their actions, which they must know deep down is, dare I say it, a sin? Do they not know that every single human being is called to holiness? Gays, as well as straights (and everyone in between), are supposed to live a chaste life, however challenging that may be for some people. The homosexual person, as well as the heterosexual person, is also called to a well-ordered and integral sexual life. Because marriage, according to our Catholic faith, means one man and one woman, joined in holy matrimony, ordered to the good of the spouses and *the procreation* and education of children" (cf. *GS* 48; CIC 1055), it is not possible for homosexuals to marry. End of story.

So, how does a traditional, reasonable, fifty-something Catholic woman, who believes in objective truth, find her place in a world that seems to be hell-bent on irrational, subjective relativity? A subjective relativity which was so eloquently described by one of the greatest minds of the twentieth century, Joseph Cardinal Ratzinger (*aka* Pope Benedict XVI), back in 2005, in his homily at the conclave before the election of the new pope, following Pope John Paul II's death:

> *"How many winds of doctrine have we known in recent decades, how many ideological currents, how many ways of thinking...The small boat of the thought of many Christians has often been tossed about by these waves—flung from one extreme to another: from Marxism to liberalism, even to libertinism; from collectivism to radical individualism; from atheism to a vague religious mysticism; from agnosticism to syncretism and so forth...Every day new sects spring up, and what St Paul says about human deception and the trickery that strives to entice people into error comes true...We are building a dictatorship of relativism that does not recognize anything as definitive and whose ultimate goal consists solely of one's own ego and desires".*[8]

This statement, along with the multitude of information I have gathered on all the important issues of our day, has set me on the path of writing all of my opinions and musings on paper. Maybe someone, somewhere, will be interested in reading the stance of a regular laywoman, trying to live her life in conformity with Nature's (Natural) Law, otherwise known as God's Law, based on Faith, Science and Reason, the very basis of Catholicism.

---

[8] *National Catholic Reporter,* John Allen Jr. September 16, 2010 (https://www.ncronline.org/blogs/ncr-today/benedict-battles-dictatorship-relativism)

I therefore offer herewith, with love in my heart for everyone, and in all humility, a compilation of opinion essays on all of the subjects that are uppermost in the minds of our modern-day society at large. I feel an inner drive to write the following pages in defense of Truth and Reason, which, I hope, any reasonable, truth-seeking person, regardless of their faith/belief system and personal philosophy, can respect and ponder on, without resorting to bullying tactics to shut me down and rob me of my freedom of expression.

Chapter One

On Homosexuality and Transgenderism

O my God, I love thee above all things with my whole heart and soul because Thou art all good and worthy of all love. I love my neighbor as myself for the love of Thee. I forgive all who have injured me and I ask pardon from all whom I have injured. Amen. (Act of love - Catholic prayer)

"A new command I give you: Love one another. As I have loved you, so you must love one another. By this everyone will know that you are my disciples, if you love one another." John 13:34-35

Jesus answered, "I am the way and the truth and the life. No one comes to the Father except through me." John 14:6

"And God created man in his own image, in the image of God he created him; male and female, he created them." Genesis 1:27

A gay friend of mine once told me that he couldn't for the life of him comprehend the transgender movement. There are many in the LGB community who feel that the transgender coterie has hijacked their platform to further their own agenda.[1] Many in the U.K. are now calling for the removal of the letter "T" in their acronym. Bev Jackson, founder of the LGB Alliance in the U.K., wonders why the

---

[1] Piers Morgan Uncensored https://www.youtube.com/watch?v=H-6keVsIOjo

letter 'T' was added in the first place (in 2015). She explains that LGB persons are women sexually attracted to other women, men sexually attracted to other men and bisexual persons attracted to both men and women; she clearly states that they recognize 'relationships' between men and women, whereas 'T', and all the other added letters (QIS2+), are mainly concerned with "identity" and not "relationships."[2] According to Ms. Jackson, no lesbians or gays were consulted, at the time, about the addition of the Trans Community's initial to the LGB acronym. She also courageously affirms that women cannot become men and men cannot become women. She maintains that no one should teach children the fallacy that they can change their sex; it would be akin to teaching them that they could fly. If they jump out a window believing they can fly, they will soon find out the painful truth.[3]

There is currently an openly gay group called Gays Against Groomers, which was founded by gay activist Jaimee Michell, a lesbian, who is deeply concerned about the safety and well-being of children: *"Michell also highlights the experimental nature of 'gender-affirming care,' a euphemistic term for medical interventions aimed at forcing a male to appear female or vice versa. These interventions stunt natural development, may sterilize patients, and have been linked to cases of liver cancer in teens. 'Gender-affirming care' aims to address psychological distress—the feeling of identifying with a gender*

---

[2] Ibid.
[3] Ibid.

opposite one's sex—through bodily alterations, rather than therapy."[4] Gays Against Groomers is being labeled an Anti-LGBTQ+ group because they don't adhere to the transitioning agenda being pushed by the culture. Michell gave an interview to *The Daily Signal,*[5] a multimedia news organization, at the 2024 Republican Convention. She explains how the SPLC, Southern Poverty Law Center, has branded her openly LGBTQ group an "anti-LGBTQ hate group." Speaking about the SPLC's branding, she says the following: *"It classifies us as an anti-LGBTQ hate group, which is the most ironic and hilarious thing ever, because everybody in our organization is gay and we even have a few trans people."*[6] The SPLC is not the only one going after Ms. Michell's group; the Anti-Defamation League and other liberal organizations *"labeled us anti-ourselves, just for speaking out, wanting to protect children."*[7] The harassment and discrimination that Ms. Michell and her group are facing demonstrates the aggressive push against common sense that is being waged in our society.

Another well-intentioned person in this era of "Gay Rights" and "LGBTQ+ acceptance" is Anna Catherine Howell, a same-sex-attracted Catholic, who spoke out against "Pride Mass" in the Archdiocese of Washington (June 16th, 2023) and spoke in defense

---

[4] https://www.dailysignal.com/2024/07/29/splc-labeled-us-anti-ourselves-gays-against-groomers-founder-reacts-hate-group-smear

[5] https://www.dailysignal.com/

[6] https://www.dailysignal.com/2024/07/29/splc-labeled-us-anti-ourselves-gays-against-groomers-founder-reacts-hate-group-smear

[7] Ibid.

of Church teaching.⁸ She honestly highlighted the struggles of same-sex attracted Christians who wish to live in accordance with the teachings of the Church. As Ms. Howell stated in a June 2023 tweet to then Archbishop for the Archdiocese of Washington, Wilton Cardinal Gregory, "*We are not 'LGBTQ.' Our attraction is a thing we experience, not an identity we are defined by. The majority of faithful Catholics with same-sex attraction I have talked to prefer to say that we have or we experience same-sex attraction, rather than that we are gays, lesbians, or bisexuals. It is the Father of Lies, the Accuser, who insists on calling us by our sins. Our loving Father in Heaven calls us by our names. We do not want to be identified by our disordered impulses or celebrate our past sins. This is what Pride does.*"⁹ She later tweeted on her Twitter account (now known as X): "*If you experience chronic jealousy, road rage, an urge to cheat on your spouse, etc, is that who you are? Should we make a special flag for you? A parade? Or are those just impulses that you struggle with?*"¹⁰ This last statement by Ms. Howell makes me ask the following question: why does this specific part of the community even have its own flag? Doesn't the flag of a nation include each citizen? Isn't the American Stars and Stripes, or the Canadian Maple Leaf enough? Why should one part of a nation get to have a representational flag while no other group does? Should I have my own flag? How about a flag representing a white, heterosexual, fifty-something, practicing Catholic,

---

⁸ Catholic News Agency.com/news/254590/why-a-same-sex-attracted-Catholic-spoke-out-against-pride-mass-and-in-defense-of-church-teaching

⁹ Ibid.

¹⁰ Tweet @RCAnnaKate

Canadian, married, childless, biological female, pro-life, pro-science, pro-anatomy, pro-reason, high-school teacher? Maybe I should design such a flag, gather other white, heterosexual, fifty-something, practicing Catholic, Canadian, married, childless, biological female, pro-life teachers and petition the government for recognition of our minority group. We all know I would be denied flat out. But what about my rights as a white, heterosexual, fifty-something, practicing Catholic, Canadian, married, childless, biological female, pro-life teacher? Herein lies the irony: just about anyone who is considered part of the "hot-button issues" crowd gets the recognition they strive for, while the so-called "conservatives" are being shut down. So, no, I will not be petitioning for my own flag, based on my conservativeness. Now, if I were to suddenly decide tomorrow that I am a transgender, atheist, pro-choice, feminist, bisexual and anything else that is considered "hot-button issue", I would have a good chance, in today's social realm, to be recognised, and afforded just about any flag I would want.

On the subject of flags, quite a while back, the LGB community decided to appropriate for themselves the universal Judeo-Christian symbol of God's promise to Noah of never inflicting another deluge to wipe out humanity: an amazing kaleidoscope of colors in the sky, the rainbow. Beholding this wondrous celestial myriad of red, orange, yellow, green, blue, indigo and violet fills one with awe, at any age. So, okay, the rainbow is now a symbol of gay pride ("pride" being one of the seven deadly sins, by the way). Ever since the LGB circle decided to adopt the rainbow as their banner, the symbolism of said rainbow is no longer up for debate. I do not wish to harm this community in any way, shape or form; at the same time, I do not wish to promote the gay agenda by espousing a gay symbol; I leave that to the gay community. A few years back, I somehow disengaged myself very quietly from sporting a rainbow-coloured decal on my school computer, without ever saying a word. It seems nobody noticed my lack of being a "visual ally". Same story in my home surroundings; I will not wilfully keep any rainbow-coloured symbols, however decorative or practical the object may be. If I did so, I would effectively be living a lie. Most well-known stores I shop at have huge rainbow displays in their front aisles and shop windows. Many of these displays are actually aimed at children. Society is effectively grooming children to be brought up in the current cultural contagion of transgenderism and anything LGB (LGBTQ2S+). Children are naturally drawn to beautiful pastel colors and rainbows; therefore, it's fairly easy to indoctrinate them in the LGBTQ agenda, from the crib. I once saw a six-month-old babe in arms sporting LGBT baby clothes, which were obviously bought by the young mother holding the infant. This child will grow up in the prevailing culture it lives in, be led to believe that men having anal sex with men is normal and good, be raised in the erroneous belief that lesbian sexual pleasure is something pure and beautiful, be taught that sexual identity is subjective, and be taught to deny science and anatomy. This child will use phrases like "sex assigned at birth", which is a fallacy. Sex is never "assigned"; it is scientifically observed and stated, based on the newborn's genitalia. Sexual characteristics are binary and observable. For a society which, for decades, accused religions of disregarding science and clinging to religious beliefs, it is

Chapter One: On Homosexuality and Transgenderism

now, ironically, first in line to deny the scientific, genetic, anatomical and biological reality of males and females. The current society's blind subjectivity contradicts any and all genetic and scientific data, in order to reinvent sexual distinctions, as we know them. This is a new form of slavery to the cultural rhetoric being spouted by a loud and forceful dictatorial elite, posing as justice and equality seekers. The next generation is being groomed in this social contagion, to the point where they will unabashedly affirm that God is wrong and that he makes mistakes.

As for me, I want to live in conformity with my beliefs, which are grounded in the Catholic Church's moral teaching. I will not be a party to condoning or advocating pride for homosexual acts (or any other act that goes against God's commandments), even though I have love and compassion in my heart for all persons. The Church condemns actions of hate, violence or aggression against anyone, including against homosexual and so-called transgender persons. This being said, even though we do not condemn the homosexual, or transgender, person, we are not called to condone, to promote, to affirm or to agree with whatever goes against our belief. Herein lies the basis for freedom of religion and freedom of expression. It works both ways. For example, people have the freedom to disagree with my belief that a man is a man and a woman is a woman, and I reciprocally should have the freedom to disagree with someone's belief that a man can become a woman and a woman can become a man. Chastising me for my belief is a direct violation of my freedom of expression, and, in my case, a direct violation of my freedom of religion as well, for I firmly believe that God created us male and female and that these two sexes are different and complement each other.

Now, many people say that the Catholic Church is "against" homosexual persons. This is categorically false. Holiness and the path towards holiness is for everyone. We are all called to holiness, which is exactly what the Catholic apostolate called COURAGE strives to teach its members. In 1980, a Catholic priest by the name of John Harvey founded COURAGE at the behest of His Eminence Terence Cardinal Cooke, then Archbishop of New York. The Cardinal wanted to pastorally help members of his flock who were experiencing same-sex attractions, yet wanted to live in conformity with the Church's teachings on homosexuality and live a chaste life. This outreach program was a tangible way of addressing this issue. The Holy See, under the pontificate of Pope Saint John Paul II, endorsed this endeavor, in 1994. Canonical status was granted in 2016, making it the only canonically-approved apostolate of its kind.[11] The moral teachings of the Church must always be told in truth and love; there must be no condemnation whatsoever of the person's predilection for certain behaviors. This is exactly what this apostolate tries to achieve, through its ministry: *"From the beginning, Courage has truthfully explained the Church's teachings with great compassion, making sure to speak positively of God's love for his beloved children and his desire for each of them to fulfill a unique role in his plan for*

---

[11] https://www.Catholicnewsagency.com/news/258771/Catholic-same-sex-attraction-support-ministry-courage-conference

Chapter One: On Homosexuality and Transgenderism

salvation. God does not care about orientation, he cares about holiness. God does not ask for immediate perfection, he asks us to grow in holiness each day."[12] The method used to attain holiness for persons with same-sex attraction is to highlight living a chaste life and by promoting a life dedicated to Christ. COURAGE also promotes a spirit of fellowship and strong bonds of sincere and pure friendships. This apostolate adheres to the Catholic Catechism (CCC, 2358)[13] of calling for "respect, compassion and sensitivity" toward people of same-sex attraction. In addition to COURAGE, families and friends have the benefit of ENCOURAGE, an extension of COURAGE, which helps them deal with the reality of their loved one's challenges in trying to live a chaste life. There are now 175 chapters of COURAGE and 75 chapters of ENCOURAGE throughout the world,[14] who help, with love, compassion and the truth of the gospel, thousands of people struggling with same-sex attractions, who want to live their lives in accordance with the teachings of their faith.

I also, as a heterosexual Catholic woman, want to live my life in accordance with my faith and with the teachings of the Catholic Church. I believe in complementarity: according to the Book of Genesis (2:22-24), God created a companion (Eve, a woman) for Adam (a man). From that union, new life was created through the sexual act of said complementarity. No matter how long two men or two

---

[12] Ibid.

[13] Catechism of the Catholic Church, (§2358): https://www.vatican.va/archive/ENG0015/_INDEX.HTM

[14] https://www.Catholicnewsagency.com/news/258771/Catholic-same-sex-attraction-support-ministry-courage-conference

women engage in non-complementary sexual acts, there will not be new life issuing forth. This is basic biological, anatomical, genetic, medical science. Even atheists can comprehend this. If we can understand the "lock-and-key" metaphor, we can understand the male/female sexual union procreative act. I am not committing any sin of violence against anyone in proclaiming this objective truth. On the contrary, it is I who suffers at the hands of those who do not want to hear this truth. This is when the dictatorship of relativism kicks in: people nowadays believe what they want to believe. Their desires dictate their beliefs. The more like-minded people they gather around them to proclaim their version of the truth emboldens them to proclaim their "truth" loud enough in order to cow those who stick to objective truth and dare to try to oppose their false "truth".

The whole transgender issue has flourished amazingly fast in the past few years. It is everywhere and it targets young people through a veritable social media bombardment. I have taught quite a few LGB/Transgender students and worked with a few LGB/Transgender colleagues, some of whom were on a quest of "self-discovery" and "questioning their identity". Some kids were actually on hormone medications. One colleague went all the way to sex-reassignment surgery. It is very difficult to comprehend how an individual can be so very desperate, to the point of choosing elective double mastectomy or full castration. I feel compassion for the poor soul who undergoes such a traumatic experience. Even though I disagree with such irreversible life-altering decisions (one should take the

Chapter One: On Homosexuality and Transgenderism

time to read up on the actual medical descriptions of each surgery),[15] I insist on the person being respected as a human being, regardless of their painful decisions. I always firmly proclaim the respect of each and every student in my classroom, no matter who they are or what they believe, and I do not tolerate any sign of disrespect for anyone, from anyone, either way. While I will demand and demonstrate respect for a gay/transgender student, I will not pin a miniature rainbow flag on my blouse or a transgender decal on my computer. We can all be respectful of our fellow human beings without espousing, affirming and/or promoting their views.

Now, with regards to people undergoing gender transitioning, there are thousands upon thousands of people who identify as transgender/non-binary in the U.S.[16] and Canada[17] and who go through gender-affirming "care". You will have noticed by now that I put the word "care" in quotation marks, given that the type of so-called "care" that transitioners receive is anything but. They are, in effect, being experimented upon by the medical community, since there is not sufficient data on this matter. In fact, there are many people who have regretted having embarked on the irreversible route of so-called "gender-affirming care". Amidst this transgender population are what is termed "detransitioners": persons who regret having undergone transgender affirming "care". Four cases in point are Chloe

---

[15] https://americanmind.org/salvo/genital-mutilation-for-the-masses/
[16] https://www.pewresearch.org/short-reads/2022/06/07/about-5-of-young-adults-in-the-u-s-say-their-gender-is-different-from-their-sex-assigned-at-birth/
[17] https://www150.statcan.gc.ca/n1/daily-quotidien/220427/dq220427b-eng.htm

Cole[18] in California, Prisha Mosley[19] in North Carolina, Soren Aldaco in Texas[20] and Cristina Hineman[21] in New York. All four young ladies are regretting their foray in transitioning to another sex and are now suing the medical establishment for the lack of true care that they needed for their gender dysphoria condition (when one's gender identity does not match one's sex registered at birth). Another person who is very vocal about this whole issue is Oli London, author of the book *Gender Madness - One man's devastating struggle with WOKE ideology and his battle to protect children (2023)*.

Mr. London gave an interview to EWTN News Nightly,[22] in which he clearly explained his stance on this issue, following years of transitioning treatments and living as a transgender female. He has since regretted this state of affairs and is valiantly trying to warn everyone about the wrongness of succumbing to the prevailing gender ideology, specifically as regards children and minors.

There is also one particularly heartbreaking story involving a young woman named Daisy Strongin.[23] She was another victim of the transgender ideology. Growing up in Elmhurst, Illinois, she always felt uncomfortable with her feminine gender; she was suffering

---

[18] https://www.realclearpolitics.com/video/2023/07/27/de-transitioner_chloe_cole_tells_congress_let_me_be_your_final_warning

[19] https://www.iwf.org/2023/08/04/detransitioners-iwf-identity-crisis-sue-healthcare-professionals

[20] Ibid.

[21] https://www.iwf.org/identity-crisis-stories/cristina-hineman/

[22] https://www.youtube.com/watch?v=map2kKDhxY8

[23] https://www.iwf.org/identity-crisis-stories/daisy-strongin/

Chapter One: On Homosexuality and Transgenderism 29

from gender dysphoria and did the unthinkable when she was eighteen years old: puberty blockers/hormone therapy regimen and, ultimately, a double mastectomy. She started to regret the entire episode when she met a man, fell in love, and got married. The desire for children grew very strong in her heart. She is currently married and has two lovely children. Her deepest regret is not having been able to breastfeed her babies. She regrets having a deep (masculine) voice and scars instead of breasts, for the rest of her life. What she went through is irreversible. Her story is well documented on the Independent Women's Forum.[24] I recommend reading, and viewing, her story, in order to fully appreciate, in detail, everything this sweet woman went through. The medical establishment failed her, as did many others, in her time of need.

Some of the main reasons for transitioners' post-operation regret are the medical facts of being potentially sterile for the rest of their lives because of imposed hormonal treatments/imbalances (or outright castration in men), being unable to breastfeed their potential future offspring (double mastectomies of otherwise healthy female breasts in girls), being in constant physical pain and having to be dependent on medications, possibly for the rest of their lives.

A perfect example of this is Lois Cardinal, a Canadian Indigenous male who underwent sex reassignment surgery over ten years ago. Lois Cardinal has requested euthanasia (which was denied), because of agonizing pain following transgender surgery: *"Cardinal underwent a vaginoplasty in 2009, but developed complications and*

---

[24] Ibid.

quickly regretted the procedure... told DailyMail.com that ... feels constant pressure, pain and discomfort now, many years after the original surgery. The difficult procedure involves inverting the penis into a neo-vagina. Most recipients suffer pain and discomfort afterward, according to a recent study[25] from the University of Florida."[26] Lois Cardinal is meanwhile talking publicly about the whole ordeal on various platforms.[27]

More and more courageous men and women are stepping up and vocalizing their regret publicly in order to stop the legal medical mutilation of adolescents across North America, in this unimaginable ideology that is overtaking the current generation via social media and school systems. Parents need to inform themselves about what is going on in their children's lives, especially what they are learning in school.

Which brings us to the recent case in Geneva, Switzerland, where a school got involved in the case of the parents of a sixteen-year-old girl who suffers from gender dysphoria. The Swiss authorities, with the collaboration of the girl's school, removed the girl from

---

[25] https://www.dailymail.co.uk/news/article-12312219/Trans-surgery-nightmares-revealed-81-endure-pain-five-years-gender-change-procedures-half-say-having-sex-painful-left-incontinent-survey-shows.html

[26] https://www.dailymail.co.uk/news/article-12349523/Trans-indigenous-Canadian-slams-doctors-denying-euthanasia-request-saying-death-free-agony-surgically-built-vagina.html

[27] https://globalnews.ca/video/10280361/alberta-trans-woman-shares-regrets-over-bottom-surgery-what-have-i-done

Chapter One: On Homosexuality and Transgenderism 31

her parents' custody and placed her in a government shelter, where she has been living for over a year, because said parents refused to place her on puberty blockers: *"The case, currently unfolding in Swiss courts, centers on parents who responded to the mental health struggles of their daughter, who expressed "gender confusion," with care and support, including obtaining mental health care. Concerned that their daughter was being pushed to make hasty and potentially irreversible decisions, they declined "puberty blockers" and explicitly rejected her school's attempt to "socially transition" her. The school disregarded the parents' explicit instruction. They then faced an alliance of the school, the LGBT-Lobby Organization "Le Refuge," and the Swiss Child Protection Agency, who brought a case against them in court. "And that has meant for us many sleepless nights, a lot of deep pain, and a sense of hopelessness," the father said."*[28]

This case is garnering worldwide attention, at this very moment, with the likes of Elon Musk, Tesla CEO and owner of "X", formerly known as Twitter, who is weighing in on this particular nightmare: *"This is insane. This suicidal mind virus is spreading throughout Western Civilisation"*[29] A second figure vocalizing dissent is Kellie-Jay Keen, a militant feminist advocate and women's rights campaigner in the UK, who says she sees *"a global push to destroy families and access our children. The erasure of female language, particularly around motherhood is part of this. Mothers are the protectors of children, fathers are the protectors of families. The state does not know or*

---

[28] https://adfinternational.org/news/elon-musk-reaction-daughter-separated-switzerland

[29] Ibid.

love our children better than parents ... Similar stories of state kidnap of children who have parents who recognise the harm of the quasi-religious authoritarian cult of trans have been reported in Canada, USA, Australia and I suspect many have gone unreported elsewhere...Parents must not sleepwalk into surrendering our most important duty, protecting our children. Trust your instincts and talk to your children."[30]

Another well known figure in the UK is Amy Gallagher, a British Mental Health Nurse and Psychotherapist, in the National Health Service, who had been selected as the Social Democratic Party candidate for the London mayoral election in early 2024. This is the person who sued the Portman Clinic (part of The Tavistock and Portman NHS Foundation Trust), in 2022, who, she claimed, were promoting critical race theory in its classes, while she was in the final stages of her two-year course in forensic psychology.[31] On the Geneva case, she says: "*This case is terrifying. These parents have had their child taken from them by a State that is captured by gender ideology. I trust in faith and hope that the parents, with support from ADF International*[32] (Alliance Defending Freedom International), *will convince the legal authorities in Switzerland that this is not the path to take and the child is united with her parents swiftly. The Swiss authorities should take into account the outcomes of the Cass Report*[33]

---

[30] Ibid.
[31] https://theweek.com/news/society/958093/what-is-critical-race-theory
[32] https://adfinternational.org/
[33] https://www.bbc.com/news/health-68863594

Chapter One: On Homosexuality and Transgenderism   33

(which spearheaded Britain and Scotland's pause of hormone blockers for minors) *and the increasing view that affirmation of transgenderism is dangerous.*"[34] It is crucial to have as many people as possible publicly opposing this ideology. At ADF International,[35] this is just one of the many cases they are involved in. I encourage everyone to consult their website, in order to better understand the challenges facing today's society and what can be done to foster justice and truth.

Schools taking over young minds is not limited to Switzerland. Are parents aware of what is transpiring in American school libraries, as we speak? Do they know that books describing homosexual acts and oral sex techniques, with accompanying pictures, are stacking the shelves in elementary schools and being taught to their children as part of the curriculum? One school in Virginia decided to remove these types of books from their library after a detailed complaint from a parent.[36] Had there not been any complaint, the books could possibly still be available to students in that school. "*The effort to ban sexually explicit content from public school libraries isn't unique to Spotsylvania County, Virginia ... Parents and teachers around the country recently have questioned the placement of explicit books in school libraries that romanticize sexual abuse and describe or picture intimate sexual acts.*"[37] This is why it is so very important

---

[34] https://adfinternational.org/news/elon-musk-reaction-daughter-separated-switzerland

[35] https://adfinternational.org/

[36] https://www.dailysignal.com/2023/03/29/virginia-school-district-removes-14-sexually-explicit-books/

[37] Ibid.

for parents to get involved in the lives of their children and not to let themselves be intimidated by the reigning ideologies.

Speaking from personal experience, when I was fourteen, in Grade 9 gym class (a mandatory course), back in the early eighties, the teacher showed a "sexual health" video, as part of Sex Education. The video in question had been produced by high school students and was apparently being showcased in local high schools. The gist of the video was that teenagers had to use contraception in order to avoid unwanted pregnancies. That was the entire message! There was no mention whatsoever of morality or of abstinence; they did not even address the danger of sexually transmitted diseases. The entire event was branded as "sexual responsibility". As soon as I arrived home, I told the entire story to my mother. She advised me to excuse myself from class if the teacher continued in this vein. And yes, the very next day, more of the same was being taught. I actually gathered enough nerve to approach her and ask her to be excused on the basis that the message conveyed by the video did not agree with my own view and beliefs on the matter. She agreed to let me leave class, whereupon I called my mom (on the pay phone in the school's lobby) to discuss the matter with her. As fate would have it, I had been unknowingly nursing an infection in my lungs for many days and was too sick to return to school the following week. In fact, I missed an entire month of school, being treated in the local children's hospital for a quite tenacious form of pneumonia. Upon my return to school, one girl told me that she thought I had skipped school the entire month in order to miss Sex Ed. I merely said no, that I had been in hospital. In fact, I never spoke about my opinions

Chapter One: On Homosexuality and Transgenderism   35

regarding so-called "sex education". I did not have the capacity of eloquently expressing myself at fourteen, that I now have in my fifties.

I wonder how many students nowadays tell their parents what goes on in school? I recently asked a teaching colleague of mine if her daughter had told her about the LGBTQ posters lining the walls in her high school and the answer was a resounding "no". My colleague had absolutely no clue that the high school where her daughter was being educated was a hotbed of LGBTQ ideology, both verbally and pictorially; she had never even visited her daughter's school. She assumed that since the school was "Catholic", everything was fine. She did not know that there were posters showing two adolescent girls kissing each other, open-mouthed, with tongues touching. Same premise with two teenage boys, and, lastly, a poster of a newborn baby, wearing a hospital bracelet with the word "homosexual" on it.

Bearing this in mind, I keep learning something new every day with respect to the transgender ideology, which basically goes beyond reason. I found out recently that there is now a serious push for "chestfeeding" in the United States (which pretty much means that Canada is next in line in its usual "follow the leader" mode): *"The Centers for Disease Control and Prevention has issued official guidance for "nonbinary" people on how to "chestfeed" infants."*[38] It seems that drugs such as *"metoclopramide is sometimes used to try*

---

[38] https://www.dailysignal.com/2023/07/07/cdcs-chestfeeding-guidance-reveals-administrative-states-latest-mutilation-of-west/

and increase milk supply (galactagogue),"[39] to help biological males who identify as females "make" transgender "milk" in order to chestfeed/breastfeed infants. According to the National Library of Medicine: "*Metoclopramide is a medication that has been used to treat gastrointestinal (stomach / bowel) motility issues, for nausea and vomiting caused by surgical operations, chemotherapy, or pregnancy, and to help with lactation. This medication has been sold under brand names such as Reglan®, Maxolon® or Metozolv ODT®*".[40] We all have to wonder about the safety of these drugs, which are known to cross over into the "milk", thus into the infants, such as Domperidone, which "*can pass into breast milk in small amounts and can sometimes give babies an irregular heartbeat as a result*".[41]

Now, even though respect for others is important, we must absolutely care for the defenseless and vulnerable among us who have no voice. The baby suckling at a man's chest for life sustaining milk has no clue that he/she might be ingesting something that is harmful to his/her health. We therefore have to be the voice of reason, based on scientific and medical facts, that are frankly far more important than an ideology that panders to the whims and desires of, let's face

---

[39] https://www.dailysignal.com/2023/07/07/man-begs-funds-doctor-can-help-him-make-transgender-mi/
[40] https://www.ncbi.nlm.nih.gov/books/NBK582840/
[41] https://local21news.com/news/nation-world/cdc-says-trans-people-can-chestfeed-babies-in-published-guidance-critics-warn-of-health-risks-breastfeed-breast-breastfeeding-infant-child-baby-chestfeeding-centers-disease-control

it, people who, for reasons unknown, want to establish these perverted ideas into law.

I wonder what will be the next item on the current ideological agenda. Logically, I guess the next step would be the complete eradication of grammar gender pronouns as a whole, as well as nouns indicating familial ties; no more usage of the following nouns: mother, father, aunt, uncle, grandma, grandpa, wife, husband, girlfriend, boyfriend, niece, nephew, woman, man, girl, boy, etc… Why bother having such pronouns as she, he, his, hers, him, her, etc… if gender doesn't matter? Why not whittle down every single language to mere grunts while we're at it? Maybe wives would prefer to squawk their way through trying to introduce their husbands without using male-oriented nouns and pronouns. Maybe husbands would prefer pounding their chests with their fists to mutely assert their masculinity, just like Tarzan, the ape man, did, back in those 1930's movies, which would pretty much seem to be the best way to communicate going forward. Surely the language police couldn't object to non-verbal communication, could they? What about the clothing/fashion industry? No more dresses and skirts, three-piece suits and ties. Let's all wear burlap bags over our bodies and be done with it. Let's get rid of the billion-dollar cosmetics industry. No more makeup for anybody. And on and on it goes. If sexual identity and gender is supposed to be fluid, why bother having any of it. Let's all be a mere cog in the assembly-line of life. Hey, this sounds like a good basis for a dystopian novel; I'll have to look into this possibility for my next book.

In the meantime, let me get back to what I believe is the problem with what is going on in society lately. Respect for our fellow man isn't good enough; the LGB and Trans communities demand affirmation. This is a form of dictatorship. I am often being imposed upon to either adopt the current ideology that seems to be prevailing everywhere or be silently subjected to it. I am either compelled to say things that I do not want to say, or forced to silently listen to falsehoods. And, we all know, that to be silent, is, in effect, to be complicit. I am intimidated into using language that affirms actions that my religious beliefs oppose. I am being bullied with veiled (and not so veiled) threats of what could be a potential outcome if I don't toe the line. This is a far cry from being respected. I am supposed to respect others, but am not granted the same courtesy. Where is the reciprocity? Where is the inclusivity and tolerance that they themselves demand, but do not return? Why is it so one-sided?

Personally, I don't go around demanding that everyone believe what I believe. This is the beauty of the Catholic faith: we propose, but we do not impose. It would be nice if everyone believed what I believed, but I accept that this is an impossibility. Why can't other people also accept that many people simply do not believe/cannot believe that two persons of the same sex can (or should) "get married"? Or that a man can become a woman (or vice versa)? Why is it so impossible to accept that many people believe that transgender women (biological males) should not compete in women's sports? Objective, scientific proof is on our side. We are not hurting anyone by proclaiming what has always been, and will always be, scientific reality. Why can't everyone see this? Is it so much to hope for? Will reason and objective truth eventually conquer the dictatorship of relativism that is rapidly taking over Western society? As always, only time will tell.

Chapter Two

On How We Got to Where We Are

Act of Hope

O my God, relying on Thy almighty power and infinite mercy and promises, I hope to obtain pardon of my sins, the help of Thy grace, and life everlasting, through the merits of Jesus Christ, my Lord and Redeemer. (Catholic Prayer)

When did the current transgender ideology begin? Let's face it, up until relatively recently, the very thought of a man going through elective castration, or a woman undergoing elective double mastectomy, as well as other surgeries and treatments to supposedly "become" a person of the opposite sex, (which is, of course, impossible) would have been met with incredulity at the very least. Now, not only is it met with acceptance and affirmation, but it is being mandated as a "right" throughout every sphere of Western society. Bad enough for adults going through this perverted view of their human identity, but what about children? How can doctors accept to put children on hormone blockers and other life-altering medical treatments, on the say-so of said child who claims to know what he/she wants? Does a 12-year-old know exactly what the male/female reproductive system represents? How can parents be so brainwashed by the prevailing culture that they accept these drastic medical interventions for their children? How has society come to the point of actually legally arresting parents who, rightly, disagree with such practices? Thank God for the government of the United Kingdom who, in 2024, is waking up to the dangers of these interventions: *"The government of the United Kingdom announced Wednesday that it was placing an "emergency ban" on the private prescription and supply of puberty blockers for minors, according to a press release. Both England and Scotland announced in March and April, respectively, that they were halting puberty blocker treatments for new patients under the age of 18 due to concerns about side effects and the largely unknown long-term impacts."*[1] I sincerely hope that other countries will follow suit and start caring for the health and safety of children and minors, as soon as possible.

We have to go back a long way to try to understand how we got to this point in time. As far as I'm concerned, this hails back to just before the sexual revolution of the sixties. Let's be truthful here: women played a predominant role in the sexual liberation movement. They rebelled against the so-called male-dominated world they lived in. They coveted what they perceived as the freedom of men to fornicate with whom they wanted, when they wanted. Men will have a lot to answer to God for their lack of sexual fidelity to their wives and for their promiscuity, glamorously labeled as being a "playboy". The sexual forays of men apparently spurred the envy of women, leading to various women's movements, feminism and agendas advocating sexual freedom for all.

---

[1] https://www.dailysignal.com/2024/05/30/united-kingdom-orders-emergency-ban-on-puberty-blockers-for-minors/

What the sexual revolution accomplished was a breakdown of life as had been known and practiced in the public sphere up until then. We all know that sexual immorality has been around for millenia. However, what sets us apart from the past is that nowadays, sexual immorality is hailed publicly as a good thing, as something to be applauded, affirmed and paraded through the streets, as something to be enshrined in law. Before this permissive era, sins had always existed and abounded, but were something to be hidden and to be ashamed of. Such is the nature of man that instead of stopping the sin and converting to a better life, he wants to continue sinning in the full light of day (so to speak) and be affirmed in his sin. Being affirmed justifies his behavior and the sin thus flourishes and abounds, perpetuating itself no end.

What sexual liberation instilled in the mind of society is that sex is not important from an anthropological viewpoint (think about it; if we all stopped procreating, humans would be extinct within fifty years or so). Sex is deemed merely as an appetite that needs to be sated, a biological function that needs to be exercised, devoid of any deeper meaning or of deeper repercussions. Just look at the July 2024 comment that American Secretary of Transportation Pete Buttigieg made about men being "more free" in a country with access to abortion and birth control.[2] This comment reflects the mindset of sex being merely recreational, without responsibilities attached.

---

[2] https://www.foxnews.com/politics/buttigieg-comment-men-free-access-abortion-deeply-troubling-pro-lifers

When we disassociate sex from its primary purpose (the God given gift of unitive and procreative love between one man and one woman, united in holy matrimony, resulting in the issuing forth of new life), it is relegated to the simple act of satisfying an urge (one-night stands were very popular at one point). No past, no future, no heartache, no responsibility. This disconnect between sex, love and responsibility fostered the notion that sex is only a necessary physical act of pleasure, but not a necessary act of assuring our future society. This mindset therefore, eventually, and logically, spilled over into the insidious, erroneous belief that sexual identity therefore doesn't matter. After all, if pleasure and self-assertion are the only ends in sight, who cares if the sexual act is between two (or more) men or between two (or more) women? Who cares if a girl/woman undergoes life-altering surgeries in order to transition into a boy/man (effectively rendering her sterile, in most cases,[3] since the goal here is most certainly not reproduction). Same thing for the boy/man who is castrated in order to transition into a girl/woman. The mentality behind sexual freedom has fostered a complete disintegration of the concept of the importance and true meaning of gender identity and sex, paving the way for such procedures as medical surgeries to "reassign sex".

I personally believe that "sex reassignment" surgeries (previously termed as sex change operations back in the nineteen seventies) should never have been allowed in the first place. How could medical doctors betray the Hippocratic Oath (promising to harm no one) they took by mutilating human beings under the pretext of "helping"

---

[3] https://americanmind.org/salvo/genital-mutilation-for-the-masses/

Chapter Two: On How We Got to Where We Are

them be who they want to be? I believe that some medical doctors have what is known as a "God complex", and they have the perfect opportunity of exercising a megalomaniacal streak of playing God, capitalizing on the confusion of their trusting patients and effectively using them as guinea pigs. By opening the door to sex transition surgeries on adults back in the seventies, the medical field was opening a window for the same surgeries on minors. And this is exactly what was achieved by the year 2024. Children being mutilated by medical professionals. Legal child abuse. Advocated by the highest representatives of the land, stating on national television that "gender-affirming care" is good and necessary.

I have to ask the following question: has anyone who advocates for so-called gender-affirming care ever taken the time to research exactly what the surgeries and treatments entail? Do they fully understand the ramifications of vaginectomy, hysterectomy, metoidioplasty, phalloplasty and urethral lengthening, not to mention the buccal grafts and testosterone treatments, with all of their harmful side effects, including neverending infections which ruin, rather than help, the physical (and psychological) life of the girl/woman involved?[4] Do doctors take the time to sit down with the girl/woman and describe exactly what is going to happen surgically? What the side effects and potential dangers are? What of the surgeries and treatments for biological males who wish to transition? Do they fully understand the ramifications of castration, transgender vaginoplasty and orchiectomy?[5] How about the nullification surgeries and

---

[4] Ibid.
[5] Ibid.

all that this entails, for both males and females who espouse the "eunuch" gender identity?[6] Can a child comprehend any of it? What about the parents? How will they explain to their offspring their complicity in this mutilation in ten or fifteen years from now? Do adults, let alone, children, comprehend all of this? I wonder if gender dysphoric persons are fully informed of the risks beforehand by the "caring" medical team before being irrevocably mutilated for life? Not to mention the excruciating pain that accompanies all the different kinds of surgeries, treatments and "revisions" needed to try to repair some of the damage incurred. Do they fully understand that the whole transition process requires many surgeries and potential life-long medical treatments such as hormones and anti-infection/antibiotics, for example? Do doctors tell them to wait and see if this gender dysphoric feeling is perhaps transient and that they will possibly grow out of it? That they may regret their decision later on, such as if they want to have children? These are legitimate questions that deserve conscientious responses.

Does everyone realize the enormous financial cost of all these non-essential, elective surgeries and medications, both for the recipients and for the state (tax-funded by the citizens)? Are they aware that if they later regret their transition, that they have to pay out of pocket for new treatments, medications and surgeries in the hope of trying to keep on living a semblance of a decent life.[7] Do they feel just a little bit betrayed that their tax-funded medical insurance is

---

[6] Ibid.
[7] Ibid.

ready and willing to finance their gender-mutilating "care" for transitioning, but not for their de-transitioning care later on when they rue the day that they embarked on the transgender bandwagon? Do they realize that what is going on here is a billion-dollar gender industry, which is also, basically, a legal medical child abuse industry? Does anyone care about the horrific physical pain and multiple ailments that will ultimately beset these poor misguided identity-seekers, not to mention the huge psychological trauma they have to endure? Otherwise physically healthy human beings are being brainwashed into becoming medically dependent and suffering vestiges of their former selves, for the rest of their lives, all in the name of an aggressive gender activism/ideology that does not seek the good of others, but rather the glorification of self-defining and self-identifying, the enabling and fostering of transient desires, and, ultimately, perhaps unconsciously (or not), the rejection of God. The intense push against reality, against objective truth is, in effect, a push against God and against all who try to live in conformity with God's will and design for humankind.

God allows us free will. Freedom, in and of itself, must have a purpose, a goal; it is a means towards an end. The goal, or end, therefore, must be the ultimate good. If we choose to do evil, we will not reach the goal of ultimate goodness. If freedom is itself the ultimate goal in our lives, it is no longer a means to an end; it becomes the end, thereby procuring us with a false and distorted perception of what we were meant for, which is ultimate union with God, our Creator. This explains the radical push to remove God from the public square. For example, I have heard students say publicly, in class, that God is wrong, with regards to the Church's teaching on homosexual acts. People think that freedom signifies they can do what they want. That is not freedom; it is license. If we follow their perspective of freedom, then, by extrapolation, anyone is free to snatch a toddler out of his backyard and sell him to a sex trafficker anytime he needs money. The perpetrator would merely be exercising his God-given gift of free will and freedom, right? Some people actually believe this philosophy. How many times have I seen, on television, gang members involved in drug trade, sporting a cross on a chain, hanging down their necks? Apparently, they don't wear it as a sign of their adhesion to Christ. If so, how could they possibly reconcile their actions with the teachings of God?

God lets us choose between good and evil. If we choose evil, we reject God. I don't want to be a person who rejects God. Yes, I am a poor sinner, but at least I know and admit that I am a poor sinner. I pray the *Act of Contrition* every day. I go to confession. I regret my sins and I trust in the mercy of God. I believe in Purgatory, Hell and Heaven. Hell is a place, or a state of being, that I definitely do not want to end up in. If I can make it to purgatory, I'll have a foot in the door to eventual eternal life in heaven. My goal is definitely, and ultimately, heaven, but I am lucid and objective enough to know that I am far from being a saint and am in great need of a detour in purgatory to sanctify and purify me. I highly doubt that I could go straight to heaven if I died in the next ten seconds. I try to do my best in this brief time spent in exile on earth, and I place my hope in my Lord and Savior, Jesus Christ, Son of the Eternal God.

Based on my religious beliefs, and on scientific reasoning, I do not celebrate the sexual revolution or the prevailing waves of ideological isms that are spiraling society into degeneracy and madness. I decry the current transgender agenda that is ruining the health of the body and of the mind of countless boys and girls, men and women in our society. I am against abortion (the killing of innocent, defenseless human beings, in the womb of their mothers, which is supposed to be the safest place on earth). I denounce euthanasia and medically-assisted suicide. I believe that marriage is the union of one man (biological male) and one woman (biological female) in holy matrimony. I do not concur with biological males competing in women's sports. I am not a feminist. I am an ordinary, devout, practicing Catholic woman who says plainly what I believe in my heart and in my soul about the state of the world we live in. I love everyone as best as I can, in truth and with all due respect and tolerance. I expect to be the recipient of reciprocity by being loved, tolerated and respected in return, and I believe in the freedom of expression and in the freedom of religion that are supposed to guarantee these laudable liberties for everyone, even for those, such as myself, who respectfully disagree with prevailing ideologies.

Chapter Three

On the First Proponents of Transgenderism

Oh God, I ask forgiveness for the bad that I have done, for not doing the good that I could have done, and for the good that I did, but could have been done better. (Prayer)

There is an in-depth documentary about the first proponents of gender ideology, featured on the Eternal Word Television Network, *EWTN*, which was founded by a Catholic nun, Mother Angelica, on August 15th, 1981, on the feast of the Assumption of the Blessed Virgin Mary.

Briefly, this documentary explains that the principles of gender ideology go as far back as the nineteen forties: French philosophers and writers Simone de Beauvoir and Jean-Paul Sartre, and Alfred Kinsey, an American biologist and sexologist, known as the father of the sexual revolution, all spearheaded radical ideas about sexuality and identity. The EWTN documentary in question, *A Wolf in Sheep's Clothing: The Gender Agenda (Parts 1, 2 and 3)*[1] brings to light concrete evidence about these three persons, as well as factual evidence about other key players, in the degeneracy of the social mores which they helped bring about. Given that Mr. Kinsey has been revered by Hollywood, and others, up to this day, it is essential

---

[1] https://www.youtube.com/watch?v=JPDafw3Q7u0

to know the facts about this man's forays into sexual research, specifically as regards the sexuality of children.

I have researched Mr. Kinsey and found another "researcher" by the name of John William Money. The very nature of these two men's "research" was faulty, as well as downright evil. According to the documentary, Kinsey was a degenerate latent pedophile, who exploited the sexuality of children; he collected data on the orgasms of children as young as six months! As for Money, he was misguided in his attempts to categorize genders. His failed experiments on twin boys in the fifties (known as the Reimer case) led to the eventual suicide of the boy who had been raised as a girl on the advice of Money. He too is hailed as some sort of "hero" in transgender circles. It is worth one's time to view the three-part documentary on the Gender Agenda in order to have a better grasp on how we all got to this point.

As for Jean-Paul Sartre, the essay "*The problem with Sartre,*"[2] penned by Clive James, Australian critic, journalist, broadcaster and writer,[3] delves into the so-called nothingness of Sartre's philosophy, stating that:

---

[2] https://slate.com/news-and-politics/2007/03/the-problem-with-sartre.html

[3] https://www.newyorker.com/culture/postscript/clive-james-got-it-right

Chapter Three: On the First Proponents of Transgenderism 53

> *"Sartre is a devil's advocate to be despised more than the devil, because the advocate was smarter. No doubt this is a disproportionate reaction. Sartre, after all, never actually killed anybody. But he excused many who did, and most of those never actually killed anybody, either. They just gave orders for their subordinates to do so."*[4]

Sartre's paramour, Simone de Beauvoir,[5] an avowed atheist since the age of fourteen, was a bisexual feminist, who maintained an open relationship with Sartre for roughly 50 years.[6] She was a philosopher and writer; her trailblazing book *The Second Sex* was the first instance of a renowned intellectual differentiating sex from gender,[7] back in 1949. The sum total of de Beauvoir's work laid the groundwork for much of the queer theory expressed today, according to Judith Butler, in her 1990 book *Gender Trouble*.[8]

Another documentary that is a trailblazer in exposing the erroneous ideology of transgenderism is Matt Walsh's *"What is a woman?"*[9] I highly recommend it to anyone who wants to keep abreast

---

[4] https://slate.com/news-and-politics/2007/03/the-problem-with-sartre.html

[5] https://www.thepinknews.com/2022/01/09/simone-de-beauvoir-queer-theory-gender/

[6] https://www.bbc.com/culture/article/20171211-were-sartre-and-de-beauvoir-the-worlds-first-modern-couple

[7] https://www.thepinknews.com/2022/01/09/simone-de-beauvoir-queer-theory-gender/

[8] Ibid.

[9] https://www.dailywire.com/videos/what-is-a-woman

of this social contagion that is besieging our society. Mr. Walsh is an American political commentator and activist, an author, podcaster and columnist for *The Daily Wire*.[10] Thanks to his documentary, I have been introduced to an amazing group of people, including Dr. Miriam Grossman,[11] a medical doctor and psychiatrist, in the trenches of this transgender phenomenon, and Scott (Kellie) Newgent, a transgender man and founder of *Trevoices*,[12] a group of trans educators opposing radical trans activism and educating families and politicians about the reality of gender dysphoria.[13] Newgent's foundation's mission is expressed, on Trevoices' website, as follows:

"Our mission is to warn others about the harm and permanence of medical transition. Many people are stuck with the physical, mental and social changes that come along with medical transition. We are here to give a voice, a platform & community to anyone who regrets their medical transition and work together to warn others of its harm and permanence."[14]

As for Dr. Grossman, she is an American psychiatrist for children, adolescents and adults, author and public speaker, who has written a comprehensive book on this entire subject: *"Lost in Trans*

---

[10] https://www.dailywire.com/show/the-matt-walsh-show
[11] https://www.miriamgrossmanmd.com/
[12] https://www.transregretters.com/
[13] https://sencanada.ca/content/sen/committee/432/LCJC/Briefs/2021-04-19_LCJC_C-6_ScottNewgent_e.pdf
[14] https://www.transregretters.com/

Chapter Three: On the First Proponents of Transgenderism

Nation; A child psychiatrist's guide out of the madness".[15] Dr. Grossman has studied this subject and explains it with respect and empathy, for all people who struggle with gender dysphoria, *"...the term for a deep sense of unease and distress that may occur when your biological sex does not match your gender identity. In the past, this was called gender identity disorder."*[16]

The prevailing societal mindset is to define one's gender based on one's feelings. I hear people around me say that it's normal to change your gender on a daily basis. A former acquaintance of mine, a biological female who medically transitioned to "become" a man, would talk about her young son changing his gender regularly, seeming very proud of his confusion. Small wonder that the child was unstable, given that he witnessed firsthand the drastic metamorphosis of his mother.

I have wonderful students who are presently living with severe depression and suicidal tendencies since they began immersing themselves in this ideology. They do not seem happier or at peace with their newfound "identities". They are being groomed by social media and so-called transgender experts, to get hormone blockers and what is known as "top" surgeries. One dear girl was in tears, saying she didn't know what to do. She said everyone around her was egging her on this path of self-mutilation. Young people do not seem to realize that they are being used experimentally by the gender

---

[15] https://www.miriamgrossmanmd.com/
[16] https://www.mountsinai.org/health-library/diseases-conditions/gender-dysphoria#

doctors and gender clinics. After all, there is no precedent for these types of medical interventions. There is no history of proven data to back up any of these ideas. Our young people are being used as human guinea pigs, to be experimented on. Just ask any detransitioner.

An in-depth examination of people who underwent the process of transitioning to the opposite sex and have lived to regret this decision has recently been published in book form by American journalist Mary Margaret Olahan. She is based in Washington, D.C., and was a contributor to *The Daily Signal*,[17] a conservative American political media news and commentary website, founded in 2014. The book is called *Detrans: True Stories of Escaping the Gender Ideology Cult*. The term "detransitioner" refers precisely to people who want to try to undo the damage that was inflicted on them when they were transitioning from one sex to the other. Unfortunately, some of the damage is quite irreversible. Once you have undergone a double mastectomy, also referred to as "top" surgery, it is too late to try to reverse this. Perfectly healthy female breasts are gone forever. Same concept for the irreversible damage of castration, also referred to as "bottom" surgery, in which recovery can take up to many months.[18] Some of the stories in this book are quite harrowing and emotional; be prepared to learn many unsavory facts that the secular media, at this point, do not broadcast. The narrative of how normal and wonderful these types of elective surgeries are, abound in the media. No one wants to talk about the intense physical pain men go through

---

[17] dailysignal.com

[18] https://my.clevelandclinic.org/health/procedures/feminizing-bottom-surgery

Chapter Three: On the First Proponents of Transgenderism   57

when they submit to castration and vaginoplasty, also known as penile inversion procedure.[19] No one wants to talk about vaginectomy (surgical removal of the vagina) and aggressive hormone therapy to change a clitoris into a penis.[20] How about the years of anti-rejection drugs, painkillers and hormone treatments that these types of surgeries entail?[21]

This entire cultural phenomenon is part of the so-called "Woke" culture, which is wreaking havoc with the ethics and morals which were once the rock on which societies were founded. As Virginia Allen, a senior news producer and podcast host for *The Daily Signal* cites: "*We're dealing with a radical postmodernism, and we call this 'woke ideology' because we don't have a word for it, but it really is radical, and it's all about basically destabilizing the current order.*"[22]

In July 2024, a comprehensive series I strongly recommend on defining the Woke culture, is available for anyone who wants to learn more about this phenomenon. *In Focus: Confronting a Woke World, Season One*, is available on the University of Steubenville's website (faithandreason.com).[23] There is also Jay Richards, co-author of "*Fight the Good Fight: How an Alliance of Faith and Reason*

---

[19] https://transcare.ucsf.edu/guidelines/vaginoplasty
[20] https://www.medicalnewstoday.com/articles/326590#surgery
[21] my.clevelandclinic.org/health/treatments/21653-feminizing-hormone-therapy
[22] https://www.dailysignal.com/2024/05/30/how-faith-reason-can-win-culture-war
[23] https://faithandreason.com/episodes/defining-woke/

Can Win the Culture War,"[24] who adds his perspective on this issue: "*Issues such as diversity, equity and inclusion curriculum in schools and gender-identity ideology have "awakened" Americans across political and faith divides...*"[25] This "awakening" is the basis for the term "Woke", which has spread like wildfire. Suddenly, it is very popular to 'wake up' to social injustices, in particular LGBTQ rights, racial and ethnic injustices, rights of women and 'reproductive rights', and on and on... It is better to wake up to the established, eternal truths of God and Nature and accept that we are not God and we do not get to decide which sex we should be! This seems to me to be the wake-up call society needs right now; not another protest march to continue mutilating our youth by preying on their confusion.

One of the main proponents of Woke ideology is the Education System. Schools play a huge role in fostering the current 'Woke' agenda, going so far as to withhold essential information from parents, aiding minors in obtaining medications and using preferred nouns and pronouns without parental knowledge. I once asked a gender confused teenager, who believed what she was hearing in school about transgenderism, if she had ever heard about detransitioning; she said no. I recommended that she do research on this subject before being led into possible irreversible damage. A fifteen-year-old does not realize the ramifications of undergoing a double mastectomy. She cannot see herself in ten or fifteen years from now,

---

[24] https://www.regnery.com/9781684515523/fight-the-good-fight/
[25] https://www.dailysignal.com/2024/05/30/how-faith-reason-can-win-culture-war/

perhaps wanting to breastfeed her baby, and not being able to do so because she had her healthy breast removed by doctors who did not give her all the information she needed. This gentle, sweet, confused adolescent was walking around in a state of confusion, receiving text messages and phone calls from her transgender doctor, urging her to make appointments and to make decisions she wasn't fully ready for and not informed enough about, to make. Such behavior on the part of doctors is a blatant manipulation of a vulnerable section of the population.

As far as I can see, society at large is being gaslighted by the very people who are claiming to want to help everyone. And this type of indoctrination is happening in many other spheres; not just transgenderism.

The manipulation of people starts with the manipulation of language, the rejection of morals and religion and the spread of self-idolatry, where "I" get to decide everything, from changing sex/gender to killing the innocent unborn child in the womb, because of a false belief that "I" control my own destiny. In other words, "I" am God. Therefore, if I am "God", why do I need the real God? This mindset is clearly seen, not only in the transgender culture, but in the abortion culture and in the hedonistic mentality at large.

Chapter Four

On Abortion

When my bones were being formed, carefully put together in my mother's womb, when I was growing there in secret, you knew that I was there—you saw me before I was born. The days allotted to me had all been recorded in your book, before any of them ever began. Psalm 139:15-16

She said, "No one, sir. "And Jesus said, "Neither do I condemn you. Go your way, and from now on do not sin again." John 8:11

    How did we get to the point where abortion is so widespread and revered as a "right"? I have a personal opinion on how we got where we are. Once the so-called sexual liberation of women took hold, the next logical steps also fell into place. In order to fornicate as one pleases, one has to fornicate in relative peace of mind, that is to say, free of any responsibility. The established definition for fornication is consensual sexual intercourse between a man and a woman who are not married to each other. Fornication therefore includes premarital sex and extramarital sex. It's basically a carnal union of some kind, without the benefit of clergy. Hence, to be able to fornicate as one wishes, contraception is a top priority. After all, it's difficult to be sexually active when you're pregnant, throwing up each morning, having swollen ankles and waddling around with a hand pressed to your sore back, not to mention the brown spots that appear on your facial skin, blighting your once blemish-free face. Who wants to have sex in that condition? Imagine the relief when the "pill" came on the market. Women could now have as much sex as they wanted without having the hassle of pregnancy looming large in their future, not to mention taking care of a child for the next eighteen years of their lives and possibly for the rest of their existence (yes, being a parent is a life-long sacrifice, basically giving your life for your child, and I'm all for it).

So, once women had what men had, which is uninhibited, multiple sexual relations, what did that lead to? Promiscuity. Pregnancies out of wedlock. Adultery. Divorce. Imagine all the adultery going on once the contraceptive pill was widely available. The fear of getting pregnant was no longer a deterrent from having extramarital sex (if it ever was a deterrent for some people). Let's go a step further. What does divorce lead to? The breakdown of the family unit. There have never been so many single-parent families in the entire history of society as the present time.[1]

This leads to another truth that nobody wants to talk about: the contraceptive pill is far from being foolproof. Women who are on the pill, can, and do, get pregnant anyway. How many sexually active women are taking the pill and are "astonished" to find out they are pregnant? Their pregnancy is not "planned" at all; it comes as a complete surprise. Given that they certainly do not want to be "stuck" with an unwanted pregnancy, the next logical course of action is abortion, once they find out that they are, indeed, pregnant.

---

[1] https://archive-yaleglobal.yale.edu/content/out-wedlock-births-rise-worldwide

Chapter Four: On Abortion

Let's ponder on this subject of contraception and abortion. There is a former Planned Parenthood director named Abby Johnson who is quite eloquent on this issue. Ms. Johnson spent eight years of her life working diligently for this organization. She is very honest about the abortions that she herself had in the past. Things took a dramatic turn for her on the fateful day she had to assist the abortionist in the surgical room; she saw firsthand the actual abortion taking place before her eyes, on the ultrasound screen. Watching the tiny human being inside its mother's womb fighting back against the invading vacuum-like sucking apparatus simply traumatized her into realizing what she had never fully understood before. This was the pivotal moment when Abby Johnson made the decision to abandon both her job as an abortion educator and her activism for abortion. She has since become one of the most vocal proponents of the pro-life stand in America today. On November 18, 2018, Ms. Johnson spoke at the National Womanhood's Benefit Dinner on being a pro-women, pro-life and pro-child advocate.[2] She explained step-by-step the process of the contraception plan as per Planned Parenthood. It's really quite simple; they count on women having up to three abortions by the time they're thirty years of age, merely based on the ineffectiveness of the contraception pill, which they, themselves, hand out to girls and women regularly.[3] They actually

---

[2] https://www.youtube.com/watch?v=775VuhHFCyE
[3] https://www.youtube.com/watch?v=775VuhHFCyE

count on the failure of the pill, providing them with a reason to perform an abortion, which is a billion-dollar industry.[4]

When I was twelve years old, I heard the twenty-two-year-old daughter of my mother's friend exclaim how she couldn't understand how she got pregnant; she'd been on the pill since she was fifteen years old. Surprise!! The pill doesn't always work. And, yes, she had an abortion; at the time, back in the seventies, she went to New York to have this procedure done. Her father later recounted how the doctor had to use curettes on her "to scrape out her insides" (I now assume this meant scraping out the remnants of the tiny human being still clinging to her womb) and how she was told she would never be able to bear a child; she was effectively sterile.

Most girls/women do not want or desire abortions, which explains why they all opt for contraception, believing the pill will prevent pregnancy and allow them full sexual freedom. In the United States alone, according to the Pew Research Center: *"The last year for which the CDC and Guttmacher* (Institute*) reported a yearly national total for abortions is 2020…The CDC* (Center for Disease Control and Prevention*) says there were 620,327 abortions nationally in 2020 in the District of Columbia and 47 states…"*[5] Are we asked to believe that none of these 620 327 girls/women were on a contraception method of some kind? Absolutely none of them was on the pill?

---

[4] https://www.ibisworld.com/united-states/market-research-reports/family-planning-abortion-clinics-industry/

[5] https://www.pewresearch.org/short-reads/2023/01/11/what-the-data-says-about-abortion-in-the-u-s-2/

Chapter Four: On Abortion

None was sporting a contraception patch somewhere on their body? That more than half a million women were having sex "naturally", without some form of contraception? That is very hard to believe. As a general rule, most, if not all, girls and women who are sexually active, are on some form of contraception. Which means what? It means that contraception, whichever method is used, is not infallible.

Here's another thing to consider. Whenever the subject of abortion arises, I kid you not, the very first argument that is given in defense of this procedure is always "rape and incest". Always. It's the first "defensible" argument pro-choicers come up with, without fail. Are we supposed to believe that the 620 327 abortions performed in 2020 in the District of Columbia and 47 states were because there were 620 327 girls and women who actually conceived a child despite the trauma of the crime of rape and incest that was perpertrated against them, defying the onslaught of adrenaline and shock induced chemical reactions in their bodies? I find that hard to believe. According to Dr. John C. Wilke, in an article he wrote for Life Issues Institute: *"Now for the important question. How many rape pregnancies are there? The answer is that, according to statistical reporting, there are no more than one or two pregnancies resultant from every 1,000 forcible rapes... factor in what is certainly one of the most important reasons why a rape victim rarely gets pregnant, and that's physical trauma. Every woman is aware that stress and emotional factors can alter her menstrual cycle. To get and stay pregnant a woman's body must produce a very sophisticated mix of hormones. Hormone production is controlled by a part of the brain that is easily influenced by emotions. There's no greater emotional trauma that can be experienced by a woman than an assault rape. This can radically upset her possibility of ovulation, fertilization, implantation and even nurturing of a pregnancy."*[6] (I invite everyone to read his article; he clearly defines the statistics and numbers associated with rape and pregnancies in the U.S., going as far back as 1973). Taking all of this information into consideration, how about if we mathematically cut the number of abortions by half; are we expected to believe that half of these 620 327 abortions were carried out because 310 163 girls and women got pregnant by rape or incest? Still hard to believe. Do I need to continue? Okay, let's keep going. How about a tenth, that sounds reasonable enough. That would mean approximately 62 033 women/girls were not only victims of rape and incest in 2020 (which I admit is quite believable according to yearly statistics), but actually conceived a child under those incredibly stressful conditions. Again, if you factor in all of the conditions physically and emotionally of each girl/woman, that number is still quite high (a far cry from 1 or 2 in 1000, according to Dr. Wilke).

This brings us to the general truth of the matter; most abortions are sought by sexually active girls and women, who are on some form of contraception that failed to do its purported "job" of preventing pregnancy, and who find themselves with an unplanned, unwanted pregnancy. Unwanted for a myriad of reasons: financial instability, lack of family support, lack of a life partner, poor housing, too young, can barely take care of themselves (let alone taking

---

[6] https://lifeissues.org/1999/04/rape-pregnancies-are-rare/

Chapter Four: On Abortion

care of a child), not in love with the man who impregnated them, bad timing (career or education), etc…etc… So how about putting the child up for adoption? Nope. That doesn't wash either. The mindset of many women is why carry a baby around for nine months just to hand it over to someone else.

Another concern is the timing of the abortion. Bad enough to get rid of the baby in the first trimester, but imagine the horror of second and third trimester abortions. Do people even know how the late-term pregnancy is "terminated"? To enlighten those who truly don't know (graphic content warning): "*According to the website of the Red Madre Foundation, which assists women in crisis pregnancies, the method used during the second or third trimester of pregnancy is known as "partial delivery", which means that the abortionist "grasps the fetus' feet and pulls them until the lower part of the head is exposed. Scissors are then used to open the base of the neck into which a catheter is inserted to suction out the brain."*[7] This is quite brutal and barbaric. It dehumanizes the life of the tiny human being completely. And, sad to say, this is currently going on in abortion clinics worldwide.

There is a former Member of Parliament in the UK, Nadine Dorries, who recounts her experience of participating in an abortion, as

---

[7] https://www.Catholicnewsagency.com/news/254748/expert-decries-brutal-discrimination-against-medical-conscientious-objectors-to-abortion

a young nurse, of a baby boy, at 27-week gestation:[8] "*After the baby boy was 'dropped in a bedpan', Ms Dorries, who was working on the gynecological ward, was ordered by the ward sister to take him away. When she removed the paper covering from the bedpan, Ms Dorries saw the* "tiny baby boy, blinking, covered in mucus, blood and amniotic fluid, gasping for breath, his little arms and legs twitching. I was shocked to my core. Weeping, I rocked the bedpan in my arms....he stopped breathing. I checked my fob watch: a little boy had been born, lived and died in the space of seven minutes. Mine was the only face he saw, my sobs the only sounds he heard."[9] This experience shows the brutality of abortion on both the baby and the abortion participants.

There is also the 1984 documentary video *The Silent Scream*,[10] by Dr. Nathan Williamson, which documents the horror of abortion, step-by-step, with ultrasound evidence, as well as numerous testimonies from former Planned Parenthood Clinic Director Abby Johnson, including her book "*Unplanned: The dramatic true story of a former Planned Parenthood leader's eye-opening journey across the life line*" published in 2011, which was made into a movie, "*Unplanned*" in 2019. Both Dr. Williamson's documentary and Ms. Johnson's book and movie unflinchingly describe the hard reality of exactly what abortion is. To see and hear about the defenseless, tiny

---

[8] https://www.spuc.org.uk/Article/385712/Former-MP-recalls-horror-of-baby-gasping-for-breath-after-late-term-abortion

[9] https://www.spuc.org.uk/Article/385712/Former-MP-recalls-horror-of-baby-gasping-for-breath-after-late-term-abortion

[10] https://www.youtube.com/watch?v=hstRrYsbffM

Chapter Four: On Abortion

human being trying to evade the suction of the tool used by the abortionist is heartbreaking; parts of the baby's body are being sucked out of the womb, piece by piece, until there is nothing left inside the mother. The child's head is usually too big to be "vacuumed" out, so another tool is used to render it smaller ("squashed", to put it bluntly). Once the ordeal is over, the nurses must piece together all of the body parts in a tray, in order to ascertain that the entire body is accounted for. This is done to make sure that nothing is left inside the woman's womb, lest infection and/or serious medical problems arise from leftover human remains inside her womb. This is done when the woman has a surgical abortion, in a clinic, with a doctor. When women have chemical abortions (i.e. abortion pill), without doctor/nurse/medical supervision, this step is obviously not taken. Where is the supposed "care" for the woman's health and well-being with chemical abortions? Just imagine the trauma a woman goes through when she aborts her baby at home. Where does the baby's body end up? Is the woman hemorrhaging? Are there human remains of her child still inside her body?

I recently watched a thought-provoking 2006 movie on this whole abortion issue; a sweet film called *Bella,* starring Edouardo Verástegui. The young woman came up with all the usual reasons for not having the unplanned child. These reasons are very real for each woman going through this difficult event. That is why we, as a society, need to address all of the difficulties women in this situation face and concretely help them and offer them alternatives to choosing an abortion which ultimately leads to the death of a tiny human being and leaves the woman scarred emotionally, psychologically, and perhaps physically, for the rest of her life. Offering alternatives to abortion is what the Catholic Church and pregnancy care centers all over North America strive to do; caring for both the mother and the child, for years at a time, ensuring their well-being for the long haul.

I can't help but think that if every single person on earth could live according to the social and moral teachings of the Church, based on Jesus Christ's own words of "sin no more", most of the problems that come about in society today would simply not exist. If everyone lived chastely, there wouldn't be so-called unwanted and unplanned pregnancies. Men and women wouldn't be fornicating; they would be living a well-ordered sexuality, based on the precepts of love, fidelity and procreation. Every generation, since the dawn of man, thinks it has discovered sex. As my grandmother used to say in her simple, straightforward way: sex and money rule the world. And boy, was she right!

Now, let's take a look at abortion from a totally different perspective: the perspective of miscarriage, which, everyone will agree, has nothing to do with abortion. The parents who lose their child by miscarriage are, for the most part, heartbroken. Their sweet little baby died in utero; the mother was longing for her baby, preparing the nursery and all the apparatus necessary for this new child. The parents and grandparents had already talked about setting up a college fund for the child to safeguard a good education; they pored through books for potential names for the baby, looked at baby clothes in children's sections in their local department store, etc…etc… In other words, they were recognising that there was, objectively speaking, a human being growing inside the woman's womb, who would be in need of all the necessities of life once it left the mother's womb, on the day of his or her birth. Therefore, the loss of this child, through miscarriage, is a very real trauma. The BBC has reported that *"in response to an independent review of care in England, the government will issue a voluntary certificate for parents who lose their baby before 24 weeks* (of pregnancy)…*The separate independent Pregnancy Loss Review made 73 recommendations for improving care for people who experience baby loss before 24 weeks."*[11] You will undoubtedly notice that no one questions the fact that we are all talking about a human being here; miscarriages are definitely the in utero death of a baby, a tiny human being. This is objective truth. There is no place for relativity here. And that is the way it should be. Imagine for a moment if the very same mother-to-be decided that she did not want the child, for whatever reason, and sought an abortion. All of a sudden, the narrative would abruptly change from being objective to being relativistic. The tiny human being growing silently inside her womb would be called a fetus, a sac of cells, a non-person, etc… and would be peremptorily terminated. This is why language is so very important; the words we use make a huge difference in our society. The abortion industry does not want women realizing that they are killing their very own children. They therefore deny the personhood/humanity of the tiny human being growing silently in his/her mother's womb.

---

[11] https://www.bbc.com/news/health-66259223

Blogger Stephen Kneale, a pastor in the UK, eloquently explains this contradiction: "*...the fiction that we are constantly being fed that babies prior to 24 weeks are not babies at all. They are mere foetuses. Foetuses that are not proper persons. Non-persons, it turns out, that we can simply dispose of if they are unwanted. This is the line that has been deemed sacrosanct and on which the abortion industry relies.*"[12]

Pastor Kneale goes on to say: "*Prior to 24 weeks, we are dealing with non-person foetuses that are legitimately...terminated, for you cannot kill non-persons. But here, we are being told that foetuses that die in utero, prior to 24 weeks, (are), actually, baby loss. Indeed, the BBC article repeatedly refers to it as baby loss. The government (is) providing certificates now to affirm this is baby loss.*"[13] Okay. Let me get this straight: on the one hand, the government affirms "baby" loss, thus, the loss of a person (a human being). On the other hand, the abortion industry affirms that the very same child is an expendable sac of cells, a non-person. So which is it? You cannot have it both ways. This relates to Austrian theoretical physicist Erwin Schrödinger's theory known as "Schrödinger's Cat", a quantum mechanics thought experiment on quantum superposition, whereupon the paradox of being both alive and dead at the same time was illustrated.[14] Obviously, you cannot be both dead and alive; it has to be one or the other.

---

[12] https://buildingjerusalem.blog/2023/07/24/schrodingers-foetus/
[13] https://buildingjerusalem.blog/2023/07/24/schrodingers-foetus/
[14] https://en.wikipedia.org/wiki/Schr%C3%B6dinger%27s_cat

Chapter Four: On Abortion

On that note, here is the rest of Pastor Kneale's commentary on this issue: "*It seems that the official position is now that of Schrödinger's Foetus. Living beings in utero prior to 24 weeks are both babies and non-babies. A death is both baby loss and the mere passing of a clump of cells. It is the loss of a living being and the denaturing of a non-person.*"[15] Pastor Kneale continues: "*It is a foetus and a baby that can be terminated without a second's concern and must be mourned as the devastating loss of a real child. The objective reality, it seems, doesn't matter. What rules is the subjective feelings of the parents. If they didn't want a miscarriage, it is baby loss. If they purposefully terminated life, it is foetal abortion. We really cannot have this both ways. Either the life growing inside a mother is a real person, a real life, a baby whose life must rightly and understandably be mourned in miscarriage or it is merely a foetus, a clump of cells, not a baby or even a person whose loss should be felt no more seriously that some dead skin cells flaking off a foot.*"[16] So there we have it; it all comes down to subjective vs objective truth. If everyone chose objective truth, there would be entire generations alive right now.

I sometimes marvel at the blatant irony and lack of coherence of doctors and nurses who, in one instance will do their very best to care for a premature baby (which is how it should be), while in another instance, a same-aged baby is being summarily aborted. Mind-boggling! Saving the one while killing the other. You can't seriously pretend that one is a person while the other is not… Every single baby, in, and out, of the womb needs to be cared for and protected.

---

[15] https://buildingjerusalem.blog/2023/07/24/schrodingers-foetus/
[16] https://buildingjerusalem.blog/2023/07/24/schrodingers-foetus/

It has nothing to do with a woman's "choice". As the U.S. Declaration of Independence states: *"We hold these truths to be self-evident, that all men are created equal, that they are endowed by their Creator with certain unalienable rights, that among these are Life, Liberty and the pursuit of Happiness."*[17] Life, Liberty and the pursuit of Happiness... Life being the very first non-negotiable inalienable right. After all, one needs to be alive to enjoy liberty and be able to pursue happiness. It is not anyone's purview to decide to snuff out the life of an innocent, vulnerable, defenseless human being. The unborn baby, from its earliest stages, has the inalienable right to Life, the same as anyone else. Which brings us to the landmark U.S. Supreme Court case of Dobbs vs Jackson Women's Health Organization. In June 2023, the Supreme Court overturned the 1973 Roe v. Wade legalization of abortion. Now, each State can rule on the legality of abortion. The Ethics and Public Policy Center has published a comprehensive analysis of all things related to the Dobbs decision: *"In the wake of the Supreme Court's decision in Dobbs, legislative and court battles over abortion have largely shifted to the various states, beginning a new phase for the pro-life movement in America."*[18]

This being said, the fight for the unborn is far from over. Pro-choice movements are relentless in their goal of making abortion a constitutional right. Pro-lifers must continue now, more than ever, to be a voice for the voiceless, for however long it takes.

---

[17] https://www.archives.gov/founding-docs/declaration-transcript
[18] https://eppc.org/publication/defending-life-after-dobbs/

Chapter Five

On Freedom of Expression and the Heroes Fighting for Authentic Democracy

"...freedom of speech is a dangerous job." Jimmy Lai, pro-democracy and human rights defender, billionaire and owner of Pro-Democracy Newspaper Apple Daily, in jail for the past 1000 days, in Hong Kong.[1]

"[T]he freedom to think and speak is among our inalienable human rights. ..." United States Supreme Court Justice Neil Gorsuch, June 2023, Creative 303 v. Eleni case.[2]

Freedom of expression is supposed to be for everyone, not just for some. I've often noticed how one-sided this issue is. Some views and ideas are publicly paraded and protected, while others are shut down as supposed "hate" crimes. Being vocal about one's disagreement with LGBTQ ideology, for example, is portrayed as hatred towards this group, which immediately silences the dissenters. On the flip side, the mockery and vitriol expressed by an LGBTQ group, such as "The Sisters of Perpetual Indulgence", against the Catholic Church, was publicly rewarded and celebrated by a sports venue,

---

[1] https://www.forbes.com/sites/ewelinaochab/2023/09/26/fighting-for-freedom-of-speech-jimmy-lais-1000-days-in-prison/

[2] https://adflegal.org/client/lorie-smith

Dodger Stadium,[3] in the U.S., in the spring of 2023. These so-called "sisters", actually men in drag, had complete freedom of expression, which was mainly to ridicule the Catholic Church, with impunity.

Another instance of freedom of expression being one-sided is what transpired at the Olympics Opening Ceremony, in Paris, on July 26th, 2024.[4] A group of Drag Queens reenacted the "Last Supper" scene, reminiscent of Leonardo da Vinci's masterpiece.[5] This controversial event sparked outrage worldwide and is viewed as outright mockery of Christians. If anyone were to mock the LGBTQ2+ community, they would be called out on their disrespect. No one would dare ridicule this community, especially on such a global scale. Christians however, are continually being mocked for their belief in Jesus Christ and the Eucharist, and the perpetrators always get away with it. As I said, it is one-sided. I will spare my readers the ignominious details of the performance, which included a child among the Drag Queens, since it is easy to look this story up on the Internet and do personal research on this subject.

Given the importance of freedom of expression, there is an organization called ADF International (Alliance Defending Freedom

---

[3] Catholicnewsagency.com/news/254461/dodgers-pitcher-denounces-team-s-decision-to-honor-anti-Catholic-group-god-cannot-be-mocked

[4] https://www.Catholicworldreport.com/2024/07/27/olympic-outrage-and-toothless-christianity/

[5] https://www.Catholicworldreport.com/2024/07/27/Catholic-leaders-join-french-bishops-in-condemning-last-supper-scene-at-paris-olympics-opening/

Chapter Five: On Freedom of Expression

International), led by a group of lawyers and legal counsels, whose national engagement is to: "*...champion the rights of our clients in courtrooms around the world and defend fundamental freedoms at national law-making bodies, securing precedent-setting victories that benefit everyone.*"[6] The focus of this organization are the following: Freedom of Speech, Freedom of Religion, Sanctity of Life, Marriage & Family and Parental Rights.[7] They represent clients and defend cases all around the globe. One case in particular stands out for Freedom of Speech: the case of Päivi Räsänen, in Finland.[8] This woman is a medical doctor, a mother of five and grandmother of eleven. She was accused of hate speech for giving her personal opinion on marriage and human sexuality in a church pamphlet, for airing her views in a radio debate and for a tweet she directed at the leadership of her Lutheran church. In June 2019, Dr. Räsänen was concerned with the Board of the Evangelical Lutheran Church of Finland's announcement that they were officially partnering with the LGBT Pride 2019 Event, hence her tweet questioning their decision. Instead of entering into serious discussions and debating the wisdom of a Christian church engaging in such an activity, a criminal complaint was filed against Dr. Räsänen.[9]

Dr. Räsänen had served as a Member of Parliament in the Finnish government since 1995 and as Minister of the Interior between

---

[6] https://adfinternational.org/our-model#national-engagement
[7] https://adfinternational.org/our-focus
[8] https://adfinternational.org/cases/paivi
[9] https://adfinternational.org/wp-content/uploads/2023/12/Factsheet-Paivi-Rasanen_Word_December-2023-1.pdf

2011 to 2015. As the executive director of ADF International eloquently stated: *"Freedom of speech is one of the cornerstones of democracy. The Finnish Prosecutor General's decision to bring these charges against Dr. Räsänen creates a culture of fear and censorship. If committed civil servants like Päivi Räsänen are criminally charged and tried for voicing their deeply held beliefs, it creates a chilling effect for everyone's right to speak freely."*[10] This case has made it all the way to Finland's Supreme Court. Dr. Räsänen demonstrated courage and fortitude in the face of such blatant opposition to her freedom of speech. Her fight is our fight. She is, in effect, facing hostility and censorship for believing and stating that marriage is between one man and one woman (one biological man and one biological woman, just to be very clear). She is facing antagonism and suppression for having tweeted a bible verse to this effect. In other words, the Bible is on trial. Imagine what could potentially come next if ever she and ADF do not win this case: the Bible could possibly be eradicated in order to not offend the LGBTQ ideologues.

Other important cases about freedom of speech/freedom of expression are those of creative liberties associated with one's career. There is the case of Lorie Smith, a young Christian woman in the U.S., with deeply held religious beliefs, who is a creative artist in the State of Colorado. Her art expresses who she is and what she believes. Her many talents include art displays, writing ad copy and designing websites. After years of working in the corporate marketing and design industry, Ms. Smith's dream was opening her own studio, in order to convey the messages she was passionate about.

---

[10] https://adfinternational.org/cases/paivi

Chapter Five: On Freedom of Expression

Hence the founding of Creative 303 (reflecting her area code, in Colorado). Her love of her craft, along with her love of people, made for a perfect career: "*Lorie designs websites and graphics for everyone. She pours her heart, imagination, and talents into her creations.* "I love being able to choose projects that I think are a good fit for me... When my clients come to 303 Creative, what they can expect is someone who cares and has a passion for their business as well," Lorie says. "Each and every one of my [designs] is a reflection of me."[11]

This passion extended itself to expanding her business to include wedding clients. Being a Christian and following the teaching of the Bible and Jesus Christ, Lorie believes: "*...that marriage is the union of one man and one woman. And she wanted to start designing wedding websites to convey the beauty of marriage, consistent with her faith's teachings.*"[12] And herein lies the basis for the State of Colorado's case against Lorie Smith. Her eventual refusal to design a website for a same-sex wedding.

Lorie Smith was not alone in having to defend herself against accusations of discrimination against the LGBTQ population. Another Colorado artist, Jack Philips, known as the "Cake Artist", was waging his own defense against these accusations, for refusing to be compelled to express his art in a way that denied his deeply held christian beliefs: creating a wedding cake for a same-sex wedding. In both these cases, their freedom of expression was being trodden on

---

[11] https://adflegal.org/client/lorie-smith
[12] Ibid.

shamelessly. They were being coerced to express their art in a way that betrayed their very soul and their adherence to the teaching of their Church, as expressed by the legal team at Alliance Defending Freedom (ADF): *"Jack, like Lorie, is a Christian whose faith teaches that God designed marriage as the union of one man and one woman. And like Lorie, Jack couldn't imagine expressing a message with his art that would contradict his faith."*[13] While Lorie Smith worked with LGBT clients on other projects, she drew the line at same-sex weddings. She knew that she would not be able to use her artistic talents to express messages that contradicted her beliefs. When discussing this dilemma with ADF International attorneys, they confirmed her fear that: *"...Colorado officials were, in fact, censoring her speech and could force her to create and promote messages that violated the very core of who she is. The fact that she cheerfully worked with clients from all walks of life—including those who identify as LGBT—would make no difference. Neither would the fact that her decision to create is always based on the message being celebrated, not the people involved."*[14] With courage and determination, and the help of ADF, Lorie Smith decided to challenge this unjust law, which denied her freedom of speech and freedom of expression, by filing a federal lawsuit against the State of Colorado in September 2016. It took years of battling this erosion of her freedom of speech, before Lorie Smith was finally vindicated: *"On June 30, 2023, the Supreme Court issued a landmark ruling in Lorie Smith's favor, protecting the right to free speech for all Americans. 303 Creative v. Elenis marked ADF's*

---

[13] https://adflegal.org/client/lorie-smith
[14] Ibid.

Chapter Five: On Freedom of Expression

15th Supreme Court win since 2011."[15] As for cake artist Jack Smith, even after two Supreme Court victories, he is being unjustly pursued a third time. He has been enduring this state of affairs for the past eleven years. ADF and Jack Philips continue to stand their ground, in the name of freedom of speech/freedom of expression, in keeping with the First Amendment of the Constitution of the United States, which, after all, guarantees this right for everyone. When a person's First Amendment right is being trampled, everyone's right can be trampled. A victory for one is a victory for all.

The latest case involving the trampling of free speech is that of New York photographer Emilee Carpenter: *"New York state law forces photographer and blogger Emilee Carpenter to create photographs and blogs celebrating same-sex weddings if she does so for weddings between one man and one woman. Penalties for violating the law include fines of up to $100,000, a revoked business license, and up to a year in jail."*[16] Once again, ADF International is stepping up to defend, yet again, a person's right to their freedom of expression. ADF legal counsel Brian Neihart states: *"Free speech is for everyone. As the Supreme Court reaffirmed in 303 Creative, the government can't force Americans to say things they don't believe....The U.S. Constitution protects Emilee's freedom to express her own views as she continues to serve clients of all backgrounds and beliefs. We urge the district court to uphold this freedom and follow Supreme Court precedent so that Emilee can speak and create consistent with her convictions. That freedom protects Emilee and all Americans regardless of*

---

[15] https://adflegal.org/client/lorie-smith
[16] https://adflegal.org/case/emilee-carpenter-photography-v-james

their views."[17] Ms. Carpenter is being forced to create messages that go against her beliefs about marriage, thus cancelling her freedom of speech/freedom of expression. This case is the most recent one to date, July 15th, 2024. Hopefully, ADF and Emilee Carpenter's battle for Free Speech will prevail. Time will tell.

These landmark cases are not limited to America. Freedom of speech is in jeopardy in their northern neighbor and ally, Canada. In America, the First Amendment guarantees freedom of expression and freedom of religion. In Canada, "...*the rights and freedoms in the Charter are not absolute. They can be limited to protect other rights or important national values. For example, freedom of expression may be limited by laws against hate propaganda or child pornography*".[18] This beggars the question of who decides what constitutes "hate" propaganda; how does the government discern what is "hate"? The local news station in my city brandishes the word "hate" on a daily basis regarding anyone who disagrees with the prevailing LGBTQ+ ideology. A devout Catholic is branded as a "hater" for not agreeing with gay marriage or teaching sodomy in schools. Theoretically, I could go to jail just for writing the preceding sentences.

In Canada, one man in particular is right in the thick of resisting the current imposition of Woke ideology sweeping western civilisation. This man is Dr. Jordan Peterson, a psychologist, university

---

[17] https://adflegal.org/press-release/2nd-circuit-rules-photographer-challenging-ny-laws-compelling-speech

[18] https://www.canada.ca/en/canadian-heritage/services/how-rights-protected/guide-canadian-charter-rights-freedoms.html

Chapter Five: On Freedom of Expression

professor and writer, who refuses to be coerced into saying things he does not believe. He refuses to be dictated to by the prevailing gender language which cancels biological reality. This man has faced persecution, trials, and loss of status and position, at the hands of what he calls "*Canada's Compelled Speech Legislation*".[19] Were it not for his courage and deep personal convictions about freedom, he might have given in to society's bullying. He has stood strong for many years, having to battle cultural ideology. Intimidation tactics are used to silence people who hold fast to science and genetics. While Dr. Peterson has no animus whatsoever towards anyone, let alone a transgender person, he refuses to bow down to dictatorial oppression of using pronouns that go against genetics and biological science. Taking this stance for reality is absolutely not discrimination or hate. On the contrary, it shows a love for truth and respect for nature. Many people support Dr. Peterson's stance and know that he is fighting for all who believe in free speech. One has merely to tune in to some of his videos on YouTube and listen to him, or read his many books, to understand who this man is and what he is fighting for. One video in particular is "*You must stand up to Woke Ideology,*"[20] in which he lays out the accumulation, incrementally, of demands, one by one, over the years, which eventually resulted in the position society is in currently. Dr. Peterson recounts how he has seen firsthand the gradual cancellation of his peers and colleagues, over time, until they were effectively shut down from ever entering into meaningful discussions or asking valid questions about important issues. As he says, by letting themselves be canceled, and thus

---

[19] https://www.youtube.com/watch?v=Xmyud5O54Ds
[20] https://www.youtube.com/watch?v=Xmyud5O54Ds

going into avoidance mode, the Woke "mob" gained momentum over time and established their reign over the culture.[21] Having studied totalitarianism for over forty years, he eloquently explains its basis: lies. Everyone lies by not speaking up for the truth. Lying to oneself, as well as to others, is the way of being led into a totalitarian way of living.

If I were to contrast this with my own experience as a teacher, I can easily understand Dr. Peterson's thesis that lying is at the root of this type of regime. I had been compelled, for an entire semester, to address one of my colleagues as a man, by using this woman's preferred pronouns. She was lying to herself, either consciously, or unconsciously, by making believe that she was a man. The school authorities were, in effect, acting like a language police, in order to enforce the lie that she was a man. I let myself be compelled. This led me to feeling that I was betraying myself and betraying God and Nature. By complying with the edicts of the society I found myself in, my freedom of expression was null and void, and I was participating in a collective lie. I was basically doing what Dr. Peterson defines as "micro-retreating". I was letting myself be canceled and railroaded into doing something that went against my conscience, through fear of, as Dr. Peterson expresses it, *"ideologically possessed bullies"*.[22]

While I admit that I was lacking in courage to stand up for myself and my beliefs (and therefore went along with this form of totalitarianism), in my own defense, I was not as well informed about

---

[21] Ibid.
[22] https://www.youtube.com/watch?v=Xmyud5O54Ds

Chapter Five: On Freedom of Expression

the ins and outs of the ideologies as I am now. Also, I had to take into consideration my personal life, mainly my responsibilities towards my family. Would I have been in a position to withstand years of legal battles if I was fired and sued for refusing to use preferred pronouns for my students and colleagues? Did I have another means of gainful employment to fall back on? At the end of my contract, I compromised and left that particular school, to find employment in another school, and educated myself over the next three years, in order to know how to better defend my rights of free speech, going forward. At some point in the future, if, and when, push comes to shove, I hope that my fear of not speaking the truth will outweigh my fear of speaking the truth. Listening to someone like Dr. Jordan Peterson is part of my self-education in this particular matter. I strongly recommend reading and listening to Jordan Peterson's views on Woke ideology and society in general, in order to be able to better understand what is currently happening in our world and how best to deal with the issues confronting citizens everywhere. He is a serious and compassionate man, seeing both sides of an issue. His calmness in the face of storms and his practical reasoning go a long way in learning how to best navigate the troubled waters of the current culture.

In August 2024, the Supreme Court of Canada refused to hear Dr. Peterson's appeals case against the College of Psychologists of Ontario's order that he undergo social media training because of his publicly aired opinions about the current cultural ideologies. According to CBC News (Canadian Broadcasting Corporation), this has triggered many comments regarding the danger of eroding Canadians' free speech rights: *"Peterson's lawyer, Howard Levitt, called the decision "a tragic day for Canada." "It seems ironic, even tragic, that he, one of the most adept persons in social media in this country and beyond, is going to attend 're-education' from people inherently less skilled and knowledgeable than he is himself," Levitt wrote in an email to CBC News. "The decision is a tragedy for freedom of speech in this country." Levitt, an employment lawyer, said the decision will have a "chilling" impact on Canadians who are members of regulated trades and professions."*[23] This case lasted an entire year and has raised issues to include whether or not a professional body is overstepping its authority when it mandates penalties over how a person expresses their opinions: *"The Canadian Civil Liberties Association (CCLA) intervened at the Ontario court level, saying that while it doesn't endorse Peterson's views, it feels professional regulatory bodies shouldn't be policing speech that is not directly connected to professional practice.*[24] Even the Conservative Leader of Canada, Pierre Poilievre, possibly a future Prime Minister of Canada, had weighed in on this issue earlier in the year: *"Another outrageous attack on free speech as regulators try to force Peterson into a re-education program for expressing the politically incorrect views," he posted on social media..."*[25]

---

[23] https://www.cbc.ca/news/politics/supreme-court-jordan-peterson-1.7288497

[24] Ibid.

[25] Ibid.

Chapter Five: On Freedom of Expression

To continue on the importance of a democracy which cherishes freedom of speech, one of the most important cases worldwide is happening in Hong Kong. It involves Jimmy Lai, a 77-yr old billionaire, who is currently in jail for having had the courage to stand up for democracy and freedom of expression. Mr. Lai could have taken the easy way out and come to America to live out the rest of his life in relative peace. But this particular individual is a man with deeply held convictions about truth and liberty. He is basically giving his life for the cause of freedom. There is a documentary on this very topic which is called *The Hong Konger: Jimmy Lai's Extraordinary Struggle for Freedom*.[26] Produced by the Acton Institute,[27] this factual presentation recounts the life of this Chinese man who has an amazing entrepreneurial gift and knack for making money. The viewer learns of his ascent in the free market system, the founding of his clothing brand Giordano and of his democratic newspaper, Apple Daily, his activism on behalf of freedom for everyone in China, and thus for everyone in the world, his conversion to Catholicism, the shutting down of his communications empire by the Chinese government and his ultimate imprisonment. A fascinating portrait of a fascinating man. His witness extends far beyond China. He is giving his life for his deep-rooted conviction about each human being's right of exercising their innermost conviction. He refuses to be muzzled and to kowtow to China's edicts of following the Communist Party's platform. And most commendable, he achieves this in complete peace and non-violence. A true martyr for our times. I strongly recommend to anyone interested in gaining insight

---

[26] https://thehongkongermovie.com/
[27] https://www.acton.org/

into basic human rights to go online and view this free documentary. Once viewed, engage your friends and family members into discussion and debates regarding democracy, capitalism vs communism and free speech. The more word gets around, the more society might, hopefully, slowly but surely, one person at a time, return to faith and reason, which is sorely needed in our world, at this time.

It is to everyone's advantage to stand up for freedom of speech. The erosion of this right is an erosion of society. The current wave of Woke ideology, covering everything from so-called "reproductive health care rights" (read "abortion rights", given that there is actually no reproduction involved) to transgender care to LGBTQ rights, among other issues, banks on its detractors being intimidated into silence. The shutting down of dissenting voices has gone beyond the limits. For example, biological reality is being vociferously denied in order to advance such dangerous concepts as physical mutilation of minors, under the guise of "transgender affirming care". Anyone who disagrees publicly with the notion of a fifteen-year-old girl undergoing a double mastectomy as a way to deal with her gender dysphoria is publicly branded as discriminating against this section of society and showing hatred. Nothing could be further from the truth. It is not hate which makes us speak out against the barbarism of legal mutilation of children. It is love of neighbor which compels us to try to save vulnerable adolescents from being manipulated into experimental surgeries and drugs such as puberty blockers. One of the most eloquent proponents of true, authentic care for minors suffering from gender dysphoria is American psy-

Chapter Five: On Freedom of Expression

chiatrist Dr. Miriam Grossman.[28] This woman has put her entire career on the line by speaking out, via public talks, interviews and published works, such as *Lost* in *Trans Nation: A Child Psychiatrist's Guide Out of the Madness*.[29] I urge everyone to read this eye-opening book, in order to be able to debate effectively with anyone who champions so-called "gender affirming care" for minors. I sincerely hope that this courageous doctor will be able to continue to exercise her freedom of expression in order to speak out in defense of young people everywhere.

Finally, most people pretty much live a humdrum routine of daily living and are not confronted with attacks on their freedom of expression/freedom of speech. It is all to the good if they are not compelled to go against their beliefs and spout rhetoric which they do not believe. This being said, they must still engage in preserving this basic human right, for everyone. No one can predict the future; no one knows for sure where they will be in one year from now, or in ten years, or tomorrow, for that matter. Being able to rely on basic human rights is important for the harmonious co-existence of mankind, and freedom of speech is at the top of the list of basic human rights.

---

[28] https://www.miriamgrossmanmd.com/about-4
[29] Ibid.

Chapter Six

On Truth, Faith, and Reason

"If you want to get away with lying, first change the language."
(Mitch Albom; *The Little Liar*, 2023, Harper Collins)

"So he did not say a word…Sometimes, it is the truths we don't speak that echo the loudest".
(Mitch Albom; *The Little Liar*, 2023, Harper Collins)

"You can trust the story you are about to hear. You can trust it because I am telling it to you, and I am the only thing in this world you can trust…I am the shadow you cannot outrun, the mirror that holds your final reflection. You may duck my gaze for all your days on earth, but let me assure you, I get the last look. I am Truth."
(Mitch Albom; *The Little Liar*, 2023, Harper Collins)

During one of my summer vacations, I took time to read some novels. One of these books was Mitch Albom's *The Little Liar*, an engrossing tale of a boy haunted by a lie he was manipulated into repeating, which ultimately condemned his entire Jewish family, and others, to death in a Nazi-run concentration camp. I am inclined to draw a parallel of the subject matter of this story with today's culture, which is perverting language in order to steer society towards a Woke ideology agenda that is introducing ideas which our ancestors would never have dreamed of.

There is a quote about *"history being a set of lies that everyone agrees to believe"* that has been attributed to Napoleon Bonaparte.[1] I can't help but correlate this observation as well with our present times. What is being disseminated in the way of rhetoric by politicians, governments and the educational machinery is basically a set of lies, by dint of perverted language, that everyone is repeating. When the repetitions are sufficiently circulated, with nobody dissenting, they soon become accepted as truth. Once this false truth is firmly entrenched, anyone who dares challenge it is effectively canceled through intimidation, loss of employment, accusations of discrimination and hatred, unwanted negative publicity, legal action, and, in a worst-case scenario, imprisonment.

The easiest way to brainwash an entire country is to change the language. When Our Lord and Saviour Jesus Christ said: *"... let your 'Yes' be 'Yes' and your 'No', 'No'. For whatever is more than these is from the evil one"* (Matthew 5:37), He knew what he was talking about. Straightforward, honest language will rarely lead to confusion. Perverting the simple truth will lead to uncertainty and ignorance, hence the pernicious path to conditioning people into accepting the unacceptable. For example, the word "abortion"[2] is used to express the killing of an embryo[3] or a fetus.[4] Given that abortions take place during first, second and third trimester pregnancies,

---

[1] https://www.napoleon.org/en/magazine/publications/a-set-of-lies/
[2] https://www.merriam-webster.com/dictionary/abortion
[3] https://www.merriam-webster.com/dictionary/embryo
[4] https://www.merriam-webster.com/dictionary/fetus

Chapter Six: On Truth, Faith, and Reason

abortions are effectively taking the life of a preborn[5] baby in its mother's womb. Now, in order to soften the push for legally killing preborn babies, the term "abortion" has been morphed into a palatable, socially acceptable term: reproductive health care. Why would anyone be against that? Health is good. Care is good. Reproducing is good. But, finally, it is a false language. The language has been deviated from the truth. Think about it. There is no "reproduction" involved in abortion. There is no "health care" whatsoever for the baby in the womb. And there is certainly no care involved for the woman who receives chemical abortion pills in the mail in order to perform a "do-it-yourself" abortion at home, alone, with no doctor or nurse with her, potentially risking her life by hemorrhaging to death on the bathroom floor. Just imagine the traumatic experience of seeing the tiny human being coming out of your body, covered in blood, and having to dispose of it somehow. This is "care"? I don't see any sign of "care" for anyone in this scenario. Therefore, the euphemism of "reproductive health care" is a blatant falsehood, via corrupted language, being repeatedly circulated through the media, in order to firmly establish the desired mindset of the billion dollar abortion industry, in everyone's mind.

It is the same concept for Planned Parenthood,[6] the organization which provides contraception and abortions for women. The name itself is deceptive, and is a lie. They are not helping women on planning to be a parent; they are providing her with the means of not being a parent. When I was a child growing up in the seventies, I

---

[5] https://www.merriam-webster.com/dictionary/preborn
[6] https://www.plannedparenthood.org/

would hear this name bandied about on television or by adults around me. I had no idea what they were discussing and I had no clue what Planned Parenthood really was. Being a child, I was innocently relying on my knowledge of the words "planned" and "parenthood". I naturally assumed that this was a way of planning on how to be a family, which I thought was a good thing. Herein lies the path of brainwashing minds by the simple expedient of false language. A benign, good, wholesome name for an organization that basically oversees the willful destruction of babies. I had actually told my mother one day, from the height of my nine-year-old wisdom, that Planned Parenthood was helping people have families. She corrected me immediately and told me that it was the exact opposite. I later realized for myself the accuracy of her reply. But not everyone realizes the truth about the perversion of language. If truth were the cornerstone of every organization, politician and agenda, there would be less confusion.

Another example of the falsification of truth, and downright indoctrination, is the transgender movement being spearheaded by an elite few, which is overtaking Western civilisation. I have to wonder why people are wilfully spreading the lie that a man can become a woman and a woman can become a man. Anyone with an ounce of biological knowledge knows that this is an impossibility. Why not content oneself with the plain, unvarnished truth? The truth of the matter is quite simple: with medical technology and current scientific advancement, it is surgically possible to castrate a man and fashion female looking genitalia, as well as alter female genitalia into a male appendage, prescribe pharmaceutical hormones to alter voice,

Chapter Six: On Truth, Faith, and Reason

hirsuteness and skin texture, and perform other various surgeries, with the end result of giving a biological male an outward appearance of a woman and giving a biological female the outward appearance of a man. This is honestly stating the reality of the situation. Instead of being truthful, the narrative being spun is that one can change their sex and become the other sex. This is a direct denial of genetics, hence, it is a lie. Therefore, not only is truth violated, but reason as well. Reason dictates that biological, genetic, medical and anatomical science is being denied.

Billionaire Elon Musk understands the notion of deceptive language and lies. I recently read, and watched, his testimony, in an interview he granted to Dr. Jordan Peterson, clinical psychologist, on losing his son to the Woke ideology, after being taken in by the lies they were feeding him: "*...Elon Musk, as he told Jordan Peterson about the time he was 'tricked' into allowing his son to become a 'girl'...he said he was hoodwinked into 'signing documents' for one of his older sons, Xavier, to go on puberty blockers...Musk's most chilling claim is that he was told his son 'might commit suicide' if he was prevented from transitioning. At this point, Peterson leaps in. "That was a lie right from the outset!" he says. No 'reliable clinician' would ever say there's a link between keeping a kid off puberty blockers and a higher risk of suicide, says Peterson. Musk agrees. It's 'incredibly evil', he says.*"[7]

---

[7] https://www.spiked-online.com/2024/07/23/elon-musk-has-revealed-the-pain-of-losing-a-child-to-the-trans-cult

There are many different ways of lying. There is the outright, in-your-face lie that is easily disproved. Children sometimes go through phases of lying and parents see right through them. Some lies have a grain of truth as their basis and are therefore more pernicious and worrisome, because they are less easily detectable. They make use of hypocrisy. Sooner or later, people get wise to this type of lie and lose respect for the person telling the lie. Others lie by omission, leaving out important facts, knowing full well that the listener will jump to the wrong conclusion. Therefore, the old adage of "honesty is the best policy" was the correct way of living one's life, for everyone. Truth, coupled with reason, is commendable, on all fronts.

Nowadays, there is a wave of subjective truth taking hold of people. They put objective truth aside, in favor of their own version of truth, which is dictated by their feelings and desires. If a person "feels" like the opposite sex, and desires to be the opposite sex, this person is being conditioned by societal norms to believe that he or she can really and truly become the opposite sex. The person's reality is subject to his or her feelings. There is a loss of objectivity regarding genetic reality.

In addition, the use of one's reason, based on science and common sense, is usually part and parcel of objective truth, which is a truth that is undeniable and unchanging, no matter which narrative is being spun, at any given time, by any given person, for whatever given agenda. It doesn't matter how many times influential people are stating that gender is not binary, that people can choose their gender and/or their sex, that standing up for biological truth is hate and discrimination, and all the other lies that are being perpetuated, the truth remains the truth, period. People are letting themselves be gaslighted by the government and social media into believing lies, and are perpetuating them no end by relaying these false messages to others.

Now, truth and reason are part of each person's lives. Very young children have an innate sense of truth and justice. Have you ever observed children having fun on a playground? As soon as one child cheats at a game, or capitalizes on someone's mistake, loud protestations of "that's not fair" make it very plain to see that they use their reasoning and sense of truth and justice in order to quickly point out the injustice and falseness of someone's action. This being said, children are children, and they are easily influenced and manipulated by older people around them. It is now quite common to hear elementary school aged children pontificating on their rights to be whatever gender they choose. They return home from school, waving a miniature LGBT Pride Flag, and repeating the narratives on Trans Rights they heard at school. They are much too young to understand the physical and psychological ramifications of such things as "top" and "bottom" surgeries and subsequent medical results following these surgeries. Today's children are being betrayed by society, and they do not have the maturity to realize what is going on.

While truth and reason are basic aspects of living a well ordered life, a third aspect is also part of the human experience: faith. I am talking here about faith in God, our Creator. Many atheists have faith in their fellow man: they are humanists. This being said, humans are not perfect. How many relationships have been destroyed, throughout history, because of human frailty and failure to live up to one's commitments? Faith in other people is not on a par with faith in God. There are three monotheistic religions in the world: Christianity, Judaism and Islam believe in one God. They believe in the same God: the God of Abraham, Isaac and Jacob, of Moses, of the Old and the New Testaments (Catholics hold that the fullness of God's revelation is given in Jesus Christ and the Most Holy Trinity). These three religions represent about 55% of the world's religious affiliation, according to statistics.[8] People who believe in God, by definition, have faith. People who have faith usually believe in reason and usually believe in truth. Yet, many religious people are believing the ideological rhetoric bombarding them daily, on the news and on social media. This demonstrates the power that culture has over society's inhabitants. The people who are responsible for enacting laws, and swaying public opinion, will have to answer directly to God for their actions, once their time on earth will be over.

Faith is a gift from God. If we have faith, it is not through our own merit. It can have been fostered in us, as we were growing up, by our parents and our grandparents. For others, they came to faith through reason, by way of science and the beauty of art, through friends or spouses, through searching for ultimate truth, or listening to a rousing rendition of Handel's classic Messiah Oratorio. Or like

---

[8] https://www.pewresearch.org/religion/2012/12/18/global-religious-landscape-exec/

Chapter Six: On Truth, Faith, and Reason

Blaise Pascal, the renowned mathematician, by way of a roadside accident, when he came face to face with his mortality. This great thinker made an intellectual decision, by way of his reasoning, to live his life as if he believed in God, by the simple expedient of a wager: *"Let us weigh the gain and the loss in wagering that God is. Let us estimate these two chances. If you gain, you gain all; if you lose, you lose nothing. Wager, then, without hesitation that He is."*[9] By the grace of God, his "wager" was rewarded with an eventual true faith in God. Whichever way a person comes to the faith, they are usually grateful to God for having come to it.

These three great gifts of faith, reason and truth, should make us wary of lies and hypocritical perversions being mandated in our communities. Being true to the truth is the only way to combat the lies surrounding us. Biological reality is not hate, nor discrimination. Castrating boys is not love and understanding. Cutting off healthy breasts in girls is not compassion. Telling the truth, in love, is real care. A man is a man and a woman is a woman; they are not interchangeable. This is objective truth. To accept, or not, this truth, is another matter; to pervert the truth, or to deny the truth, resorts to subjectivism and relativism.

In conclusion, I strongly recommend familiarizing oneself on the subject of the Dictatorship of Relativism,[10] as explained by Joseph Cardinal Ratzinger, AKA Pope Benedict XVI, to gain more

---

[9] https://www.britannica.com/topic/Pascals-wager
[10] https://www.ncregister.com/blog/benedict-vs-the-dictatorship-of-relativism

insight on the subject of relativism. Hopefully, through reason and truth, and seriously pondering what he has to say about subjectivity and relativity, readers might gain better insight into the manipulation used in society to make people accept what is, in reality, unacceptable.

Chapter Seven

On Science

"The heavens declare the glory of God, and the sky above proclaims his handiwork." Psalm 19:1

"When I look at your heavens, the work of your fingers, the moon and the stars, which you have set in place, what is man that you are mindful of him, and the son of man that you care for him?" Psalm 8: 3-4

Christianity is a religion based on faith and reason. God has given his creatures free will and the gift of reason. Based on this reasoning power, mankind observes everything that nature has to offer us. Science is defined as: *"The careful study of the structure and behavior of the physical world, especially by watching, measuring and doing experiments, and the development of theories to describe the results of these experiments."*[1] Since Christians believe that God created the world and everything in it, they have nothing to fear from studying this physical world; hence, nothing to fear from Science. With their intelligence and reason, scientists study what, ultimately, has been created by God. Many of the scientific discoveries, up to this point, such as vaccines, and genetics, among others, have been contributions from Catholics. Having majored in Biological Sciences myself, I well understand the fascination with wanting to

---

[1] https://dictionary.cambridge.org/dictionary/english/science

understand, as much as possible, the ins and outs of Nature. This being said, while it is fine to understand Nature, through Science, it is not fine to play God, and redefine Nature. Therein lies the importance of combining reason with faith and not relying on reason alone. The dimension of faith makes for a judicial and ethical use of one's reason. Many of the most well known scientists and mathematicians, past and present, are Christians, or atheists who have come to the faith through science. Their works and discoveries have been duly noted by the Church, who does not fear their contributions to the study of God's Nature.

For a long time now, society has accused the Church of being anti-science, backwards, ancient, etc... This could not be further from the truth. The Catholic Church has acknowledged, multiple times, that it has nothing to fear from Science. As an example, it has apologized for its unjust treatment of 17th century Italian mathematician and astronomer Galileo Galilei, albeit many centuries after the fact, demonstrating its ability to admit its faults and make amends. I will not go into the Church's reasons, in the 17th century, for wanting to silence this scientist. What I can say is that Galileo understood that there was nothing to fear from studying creation: *"The laws of nature are written by the hand of God in the language of mathematics."*[2] Galileo was only one of a myriad of believing physicists and mathematicians to have contributed his genius to the world. Their shining example of combining faith and reason is quite simply a marvel to behold.

---

[2] https://scriptures.blog/bible-verses-about-science/

Chapter Seven: On Science

Before delving into a list of world renowned Christian scientists and their achievements, I would like to share with my readers what the previous Pope had to say regarding the relationship between faith and science. Pope Francis had met with scientists many times, since ascending to the papacy in 2013. Every now and then, there are special gatherings of scientists from all over the world at the Vatican. In 2016, physicist Stephen Hawking, among others, attended one such meeting, to discuss Climate Change. In June 2024, cosmologists, theoretical physicists and scientists gathered at the second conference of the Vatican Specula to discuss "Black Holes, Gravitational Waves and Space-Time Singularities".[3] The conference itself was dedicated to George Lemaître, a Belgian Catholic priest, a physicist and cosmologist, who is credited with the 1931 Big Bang Theory, and whose scientific value is recognized by the International Astronomical Union. Pope Francis began the proceedings by paying homage to Monsignor Lemaître: "*...an exemplary priest and scientist*" whose "*human and spiritual journey represents a model of life from which we can all learn*" as he understood that "*science and faith follow two different and parallel paths, between which there is no conflict... These paths can harmonize with each other, because both science and faith, for a believer, have the same matrix in the absolute Truth of God.*"[4] A beautiful homage indeed, underlining the fact that faith

---

[3] https://www.vaticannews.va/en/pope/news/2024-06/pope-francis-address-scientists-black-holes-specula.html

[4] https://www.vaticannews.va/en/pope/news/2024-06/pope-francis-address-scientists-black-holes-specula.html

and science follow "parallel" paths, thus are not in conflict with one another.

Pope Francis was not the first Pontiff to encourage scientific research. According to the Vatican Observatory's Historical page on their website: "*In its historical roots and traditions, the Vatican Observatory is one of the oldest astronomical institutes in the world.*"[5] In 1582, Pope Gregory XIII appointed a committee to study scientific data. Since then, Popes have consistently been interested in, and supported, astronomical research.[6] The Papacy founded three observatories in the 18th and 19th centuries, culminating in being the first to classify stars according to their spectra.[7] Light emanates from stars, and this light can be *"separated into its component colors to form a spectrum. The spectrum reveals details in the brightness of different colors of starlight that are not visible to the naked eye. Detectors in the telescope can measure the precise brightness of individual wavelengths."*[8] Given this rich tradition of scientific research in astronomy at the Vatican, and supported by the Church, Pope Leo XIII, in 1891, *"formally re-founded the Specola Vaticana (Vatican Observatory) and located it on a hillside behind the dome of St. Peter's Basilica."*[9] Pope Leo XIII wanted to show the world that faith and science were not in conflict with each other.[10] It was Pope Pius XI

---

[5] https://www.vaticanobservatory.va/en/history
[6] Ibid.
[7] Ibid.
[8] https://webbtelescope.org/contents/media/images/01F8GF7Z3Q28EJBC051YNTMJ2X#
[9] https://www.vaticanobservatory.va/en/history
[10] https://www.youtube.com/watch?v=OM5tLK4elRI

who provided a new location for the Observatory, and, eventually, two new telescopes were added, as well as a laboratory and various programs, to expand the research being done in astronomy.[11] Footage from 1969, when Pope Paul VI visited the Vatican Observatory to observe the moon landing can be seen today, via YouTube.[12] The current Director of the Vatican Observatory is the American Jesuit Brother, Guy Consolmagno, who was named to the post in 2015 by Pope Francis.[13]

In the 21st century, the tradition of the Successors of St. Peter being interested in, and supporting, astronomical research, continues. In June 2018, while speaking with participants in a summer course at the Vatican Observatory, Pope Francis had addressed the issue of Faith and Science: *"Just as we should never think we know everything, we should never fear trying to learn more…it is through us, human beings, that this universe can become, so to speak, aware of itself and of its Maker…"*[14] The Pope went on to say that *"Driven by reason, curiosity and the enjoyment of things, scientists can discover in their love for the universe a 'foretaste' of the love that God the Creator has for His Creation."*[15] Echoing Pope Francis on this subject

---

[11] https://www.vaticanobservatory.va/en/history

[12] https://www.youtube.com/watch?v=OM5tLK4elRI

[13] https://www.americamagazine.org/issue/pope-names-us-jesuit-planetary-scientist-head-vatican-observatory

[14] https://aleteia.org/2018/06/14/love-of-science-can-be-a-foretaste-of-divine-love-says-pope-francis

[15] Ibid.

is Robert Barron, auxiliary Bishop of Los Angeles. In a video announcing the launch of his new website, reasonfaithscience.com,[16] he states how there is no contradiction between religion and science.[17] And now, our current Holy Father, Pope Leo XIV, is continuing the tradition of encouraging scientific endeavours and research. On July 21st, 2025, in recognition of the anniversary of the Apollo 11 manned mission to land on the moon, back in 1969, the Supreme Pontiff spoke with Buzz Aldrin, the second human after Neil Armstrong, to walk on the moon.[18] In addition to this call, Pope Leo visited the telescopes and instruments in the Domes of the Vatican Observatory at Castel Gandolfo, his summer residence.[19] These are not the actions of someone who is afraid of scientific advancement.

Men of faith have long thirsted for scientific knowledge. Their search unlocked the doors to amazing discoveries which demonstrated that the reality of God and his creation is not in opposition to science. I offer herewith some shining examples of world renowned Catholic scientists, who demonstrated this very concept of faith and science complementing each other, in order to quell the narrative that Christians are against science or that all scientists are atheists. Many of the very first astronomers and scientists were actually priests and religious brothers. They did not fear being led away from

---

[16] https://www.reasonfaithscience.com/
[17] https://aleteia.org/2018/07/09/bishop-barron-takes-on-the-myth-that-faith-and-science-are-enemies
[18] https://www.vaticannews.va/en/pope/news/2025-07/apollo-11-anniversary-pope-leo-xiv-speaks-astronaut-buzz-aldrin.html
[19] Ibid.

God because of wanting to understand the intricacies of the cosmos. On the contrary, their research brought them ever closer to God, in their sheer amazement of God's creation.

As far back as the 11th century, men were fascinated with the heavens above. In the year 1013, a baby was born into the noble family of Count Wolverad II,[20] in the historic region of Swabia, in southwestern Germany. His name was Herman. This child had several physical challenges, stemming from a paralytic disease, hence his moniker of "Herman the Cripple" and "Herman the Twisted."[21] From the accounts given, and from what is known about medicine today, attempts at modern diagnoses were made; it is probable that he had a cleft palate, cerebral palsy and spina bifida, and/or ALS (Amyotrophic Lateral Sclerosis) or Spinal Muscular Atrophy. As was the custom at the time, the youngest son of a noble house was brought to the Monastery to be reared and educated by the monks. Therefore, when Herman was seven years old, he was handed over to the Benedictine Monastery of Reichenau. This was a good solution for everyone. Not only did Herman learn to read and write, it turns out that he was something of a genius. What he could not accomplish with his body, he accomplished with his mind. He was proficient in Greek, Arabic and Latin. This particular monastery was a center where manuscripts were copied; Herman would translate important documents. Mathematics and Astronomy were his strong

---

[20] https://mathshistory.st-andrews.ac.uk/Biographies/Hermann_of_Reichenau/
[21] https://salesianity.blogspot.com/2014/09/saint-of-day-blessed-hermann-of.html

suit. Many works already available in these fields were written only in Arabic. Herman translated them, rendering them accessible to Europeans. In addition to his translation skills, he introduced different types of astronomical instruments, such as a portable sundial and an astrolabe, an instrument to calculate the height of the sun, as well as star charts.[22] Another important contribution was his calculations of the earth's diameter, among other things. He became a monk in 1043, and was beatified by the Catholic Church in 1863 and is known, to this day, as Blessed Herman of Reichenau. His life testifies that the monks of Reichenau, and the Catholic Church, had no conflict with science; they were in full harmony with God and His creation, contributing Herman's discoveries to the world since the 11th century.

An illustrious scientist of more recent times was Francesco Faà di Bruno, a professor of mathematics and lecturer at the University of Turin, in Italy, in the 19th century. This man had studied with Le Verrier, who helped discover the existence of the planet Neptune,[23] and was conferred the Degree of Doctor of Science by the Universities of Paris and of Turin. He invented various scientific equipment, published some forty articles on math and science as well as a mathematical formula used today and known as "Faà di Bruno's Formula".[24] The harmony between faith and science in this man's life is

---

[22] https://salesianity.blogspot.com/2014/09/saint-of-day-blessed-hermann-of.html

[23] https://aleteia.org/2018/04/19/these-saints-were-influential-astronomers-who-wed-science-and-faith-together

[24] https://www.newadvent.org/cathen/05740a.htm

Chapter Seven: On Science

demonstrated by the fact that he was also a priest. He was beatified in 1988 by Pope John Paul II. Another concrete example of faith and science being compatible.

Another figure that just about everyone has heard about is Louis Pasteur, a layman, biologist and devout Catholic. This man gave the world the process of heating liquids to kill bacteria that was latent in them; this process became known as pasteurization.[25] He also developed vaccines for rabies[26] and anthrax, effectively laying the groundwork for the science of immunology.[27] In addition to Pasteur's dedication to science, he was a believer and a Catholic. His life and writings bear witness to his faith. For example, in a letter written to his sister, he said: *"If by chance you falter on the journey, a hand will be there to support you. If that should be wanting, God, who alone would take the hand from you, would accomplish the work."*[28] When he was in his seventies, *"Pasteur spoke of the end of his journey and how it came to him "in an absolute faith in God and Eternity" and with a conviction that the good given us in this world will be continued*

---

[25] https://aleteia.org/2017/11/10/louis-pasteur-father-of-microbiology-and-a-Catholic

[26] https://www.pasteur.fr/en/institut-pasteur/history/troisieme-epoque-1877-1887

[27] https://aleteia.org/2017/11/10/louis-pasteur-father-of-microbiology-and-a-Catholic

[28] https://www.pasteurbrewing.com/louis-pasteur-a-religious-man/

here-after."²⁹ These words are those of a believer, who had no conflict with his faith and his reason coexisting in complete accord, and for the good of mankind.

Other great scientific minds are the men who basically invented scientific genetics and geology: Gregor Mendel, a Catholic monk, and Nicholas Steno, a Catholic priest. These men combined their faith and their reason in a search for understanding God's Creation. No conflict for them. Same concept for Saint Albert the Great, priest and bishop. This 13th century Dominican teacher, preacher and leader is revered as the greatest scientist of the medieval period: "*He had an almost encyclopedic knowledge of a range of physical sciences, from physics to biology to astronomy, and his own investigations demonstrated an early use of a form of the scientific method that would become more formalized a few hundred years later. He wrote treatises on general topics such as minerals, plants and animals, as well as detailed studies on the heavenly bodies and early forms of chemistry… He helped to found the oldest university in Germany, the University of Cologne…St. Albert died in 1280…was canonized and named a Doctor of the Church in 1931. He was named the patron saint of natural scientists in 1941.*"³⁰

These amazing scientists are among many others, who are household names in the fields of sciences and mathematics. How about René Descartes, "*a pivotal figure in the Scientific Revolution,*

---

²⁹ Ibid.

³⁰ https://aleteia.org/2018/11/15/perhaps-no-one-shows-better-the-faith-science-alliance-than-this-saint

as well as in the history of mathematics and philosophy...(whose) greatest contribution was the founding of analytic geometry, (and) who always insisted that he was a devout and orthodox Catholic."[31] How about Copernicus, the Polish astronomer *"whose heliocentric theory helped set in motion the Scientific Revolution from which modern science was born."*[32] Fearing ridicule and opposition from the scientific community, Copernicus did not want to publish his findings on the heliocentric theory of astronomy. It was at the behest of Nikolaus von Schönberg, a Cardinal of the Catholic Church, who had attended Copernicus's lectures, along with Pope Clement VII and other Cardinals, that Copernicus was encouraged to publish his theory: "*In 1536, Cardinal Nikolaus von Schönberg urged Copernicus to "communicate this discovery of yours to scholars."*[33]

Let us continue honoring great Catholic scientists and mathematicians. André-Marie Ampère is the brilliant French researcher who discovered, in 1823, what is known as "Ampère's Law", which is essentially the foundation of the science of electro-dynamics, after expanding on Oersted's serendipitous discovery *"that an electrical current in a wire can cause a nearby compass needle to move."*[34] His mathematical law describes the actual force of the magnetism between two pieces of wire which carry electrical current.[35] What is

---

[31] https://Catholicscientists.org/scientists-of-the-past/rene-descartes/
[32] https://Catholicscientists.org/scientists-of-the-past/nicolaus-copernicus/
[33] Ibid.
[34] https://Catholicscientists.org/scientists-of-the-past/andre-marie-ampere/
[35] Ibid.

commonly called "amp" nowadays is actually the "ampere", the unit of electrical current, which was so named in honor of this great scientist. It turns out that Ampère was a believing Christian, albeit with doubts, who finally reconciled his faith and his love of science. According to *The Catholic Encyclopedia*: "*On the day of his wife's death he wrote two verses from the Psalms, and the prayer 'O Lord, God of Mercy, unite me in heaven with those whom you have permitted me to love on earth.' Serious doubts harassed him at times and made him very unhappy. Then he would take refuge in the reading of the Bible and the Fathers of the Church. 'Doubt,' he says in a letter to a friend, 'is the greatest torment that a man suffers on earth.'*"[36] Regarding his doubts, one of his contemporaries, the French writer and historian Charles Augustin Sainte-Beuve, pronounced the following: "*Ampère's doubts subsided over time and he attained in his own mind "an alliance of faith and science, of belief and hope in human thought and adoration before the Revealed Word."*"[37] Furthermore, Ampère wrote the following in his Essay on the philosophy of science: "*We can see only the works of the Creator, but through them we rise to a knowledge of the Creator Himself.*"[38]

---

[36] https://www.newadvent.org/cathen/01437c.htm
[37] https://Catholicscientists.org/scientists-of-the-past/andre-marie-ampere/
[38] Ibid.

Chapter Seven: On Science

20th century historian and Chaired Professor at Cornell University's Department of History, Leslie Pearce Williams, relates the following in the Dictionary of Scientific Biographies :[39] "*Ampère's philosophy permitted him to retain both a belief in God and a belief in the real existence of an objective nature.*"[40] Williams details the argument[41] that Ampère used to prove that the soul and God had to exist, based on his philosophical interpretation of Kant; a simple and understandable concept of moving one's arm to make a point about objective reality and the subjectivity of one's personal sensation, or feeling, about a subject: "*The act of moving one's arm provided a firm proof that a cause explained an act and was not simply a description of succession. One wills the arm to move and one is conscious of the act of willing; the arm then moves. Therefore the arm moves because one wills it to. Ampère used this argument to prove the existence of an external world. If one's arm cannot move because it is, say, under a heavy table, then one becomes conscious of causes external to oneself. The arm does not move because the table prevents it from doing so. Thus Ampère carried causation from the psychological world to the physical world. Moreover, the resistance of the table proved, to Ampère's satisfaction, that matter does exist, for this external cause must

---

[39] WILLIAMS, L. Pearce. "Ampère", in Dictionary of Scientific Biography, Charles C. Gillispie (ed.), vol. 1, New York: Scribner, 1970, p. 139-147.*

[40] http://www.ampere.cnrs.fr/ice/ice_page_detail.php
[41] Ibid.

be independent of our sensation of it. With similar arguments, Ampère was able to prove that the soul and God also must exist."[42] Ampère's scientific and mathematical reasoning made it unacceptable for him to believe in subjectivity. Objective truth wins over subjectivity every time. Once again, the harmony between faith and science is amply demonstrated in the life of this scientific and mathematical genius. It is well worth one's time to read up on this man and on all the contributions he made to the field of science and how his faith played a major role in his life.

Another great scientific mind to have contributed to science is Cassini. Giovanni Domenico Cassini was born in 1625, and died in 1712 at the age of 87. He is considered the greatest astronomer of the 17th century, after Keppler and Galileo.[43] He was educated by the Jesuits, a Catholic congregation of priests, founded by Saint Ignatius of Loyola, a 16th century soldier, priest and theologian. Cassini became the principal chair of Astronomy at the University of Bologna at the young age of 25. By the time he was 44 yrs old, Paris invited him to set up the Paris Observatory, where he lived out the rest of his life. Discoveries attributed to Cassini are four of Saturn's moons and the gap in Saturn's rings, now known as Cassini's Divisions. Cassini is the one who achieved the remarkable feat of measuring the size of the solar system and determining the rotation rate of Mars and Jupiter.[44] In other words, this man contributed an

---

[42] Ibid.

[43] https://Catholicscientists.org/scientists-of-the-past/giovanni-domenico-cassini/

[44] Ibid.

Chapter Seven: On Science 115

amazing amount of scientific data, way back in the 17th century. Small wonder that modern astronomy called the robotic spacecraft sent to study the planet Saturn after this scientific giant. The Cassini probe studies *"Saturn and its complex system of rings and moons in unprecedented detail. It was one of the most ambitious efforts ever mounted in planetary exploration."*[45] All this being said, it is known that Cassini was a believing Catholic by the simple fact of his writings to Riccioli,[46] a Jesuit priest and an astronomer. In his manuscript,[47] Cassini not only pondered on the subject of the Blessed Virgin Mary, but advocated for the celebration of a special feast day in her honor as the Immaculate Conception, a typically Catholic doctrine and belief. Once again, it is plain to see that faith and science are not mutually exclusive.

This brings us further in our discussion of the contributions of Catholics scientists. The 18th century Italian pioneer in bioelectricity, Luigi Galvani, had degrees in medicine and philosophy and was appointed as a permanent lecturer in anatomy at the University of Bologna. His treatise *"On the power of electricity in muscular movement"* laid the foundation for the fields of bioelectricity and electrophysiology.[48] This man, like other scientists before, and after, him, was a believing Catholic. He had been devoutly religious as an adolescent and wanted to enter religious life. His parents were

---

[45] https://science.nasa.gov/mission/cassini/
[46] https://www.oxfordreference.com/display/10.1093/oi/authority.20110803100419604#
[47] https://Catholicscientists.org/scientists-of-the-past/giovanni-domenico-cassini/
[48] https://Catholicscientists.org/scientists-of-the-past/luigi-galvani/

against this idea. He eventually married, and did research work with his wife Lucia. He never lost his faith and piousness. He became a member of the Third Order of Saint Francis later on in his life.[49] This demonstrates that lay people who are devout Christians can amalgamate their faith with their reason, in their pursuit of scientific knowledge. Their faith in no way impedes their intellectual curiosity and does not diminish their intellectual capacities.

Our little historical overview of great Catholic scientists and mathematicians brings us to perhaps the most brilliant of the mathematical minds, and philosophers, of all time: Blaise Pascal. Born in 1623, in Clermont-Ferrand, France, Pascal lived only for thirty-nine years, yet managed to contribute enormously to mathematics and to philosophy. His intellectual prowess was universally recognized when he was only sixteen years old. This is when he fine-tuned his research on projective geometry, and elaborated his theorem, known famously as "Pascal's Theorem".[50] By the time he was nineteen, he had devised and built the first calculating machine, which paved the way for the sophisticated calculators used nowadays. He is the person who formulated the Pascal Principle of Hydrostatics, making him famous in Physics, for his work on the pressure of fluids.[51]

It was at the age of thirty-one, that Pascal had a conversion, so to speak, which deeply affected him spiritually. On the evening of

---

[49] Ibid.
[50] https://www.britannica.com/science/Pascals-theorem
[51] https://Catholicscientists.org/scientists-of-the-past/blaise-pascal/

Chapter Seven: On Science

November 23rd, 1654, he had a mystical experience, which led him on the path of devoting more time to religious subjects. On that evening, Pascal was in a horse-drawn carriage accident, whereupon the horses plunged to their death, over the River Seine Bridge. Pascal and the other occupants' lives were spared. From then on, he would write extensively on religious subjects, first through "Provincial Letters", then a treatise on the defense of the Christian religion, only to die before it was completed. There were enough fragments of this text to be published posthumously, under the title *"Pensées"*[52] *("Thoughts")*. Despite being unfinished, Pascal's Thoughts are regarded as *"a philosophical and spiritual masterpiece as well as a masterpiece of French literary style."*[53] It is in these *Thoughts* that Pascal's most famous passage is found; his "Wager": *"Pascal argues, on the basis of the logic of probability, that is is more advantageous to believe in God than not, since the gains of belief, if he exists, are far greater that any loss we would incur by believing if he does not exist. In the light of this, he argues that anyone who cannot believe should condition himself or herself to do so by the bodily discipline of practicing Christian rituals."*[54] Pascal actually put his own wager to the test. He eventually came to sincerely believe in God. At the time of his death, a manuscript, written in his own hand, sewn into the inside of his doublet, was found, with the following words inscribed: *"Fire. The God of Abraham, the God of Isaac, the God of Jacob. Not of the philosophers and intellectuals. Certitude, certitude, feeling, joy, peace. Oh, just Father, the world has not known you, but I have known you.*

---

[52] https://www.penseesdepascal.fr/
[53] https://Catholicscientists.org/scientists-of-the-past/blaise-pascal/
[54] https://academic.oup.com/book/36863/chapter-abstract/322075979

Joy, joy, joy of tears."[55] In 2024, Pope Francis had considered the possibility of beatifying[56] Pascal, a mathematical genius, which, again, demonstrates the absolute harmony of science and faith.

My final example of a great scientific mind at work is Francis Collins, a self-professed atheist as a young man,[57] who eventually became an Evangelical Christian believer. Collins is the physician who led the Human Genome Project at the turn of the 21st century. In his 2006 bestselling book, *The Language of God: A Scientist Presents Evidence for Belief,* Dr. Collins lays out his arguments that "*advances in science present "an opportunity for worship," rather than a catalyst for doubt."*[58] In this book, he also presents arguments that: *"... in his view, justifies faith...Collins argues that faith is rational, that it can help answer life's deepest questions, and that the challenges of the twenty-first century require a harmony between science and religion, not just a ceasefire."*[59] Furthermore, according to The New Yorker: "*Collins, an evangelical Christian, would later describe sequencing the human genome as "both a stunning scientific achievement and an occasion of worship."*[60] Collins went on to be the founder of BioLogos: "*an organization that supports the view that God created

---

[55] https://pillars.taylor.edu/cgi/viewcontent.cgi?article=1012&context=acms-2005#:~:text=Pascal

[56] https://www.britannica.com/topic/beatification

[57] https://biologos.org/resources/francis-collins-a-testimony

[58] https://www.pewresearch.org/science/2008/04/17/the-evidence-for-belief-an-interview-with-francis-collins/

[59] https://www.newyorker.com/news/persons-of-interest/faith-science-and-francis-collins

[60] Ibid.

Chapter Seven: On Science

all things through the instrument of evolution."[61] On the prevailing mindset that society has, regarding a so-called conflict between science and religion, Dr. Collins granted an interview to the Pew Research Centre, in which he stated: "*I don't believe there is an inherent conflict, but I believe that humans, in our imperfect nature, sometimes imagine conflicts where there are none. We see something that threatens our own personal view, and we figure that there must be some reason why that alternative view has to be wrong, or even why it has to be evil.*"[62] Hence, another fine example of faith and science coexisting without conflict.

All of these examples of exceptionally gifted scientists and mathematicians reinforce the reality of faith and science working well together. There is no dichotomy between religion and reason. Personally, I refute the claims that people who believe in God are incapable of relying on scientific fact. It is simply untrue to make such an assertion. Furthermore, I find it quite ironic that the same people who spout this rhetoric, are the ones who deny the scientific, genetic, medical and anatomical reality of something as basic as the difference between males and females. They throw away objective, scientific reality, and believe, or feign to believe, in their own subjective desires, which have no basis on scientific evidence and which leads them, for example, on the erroneous path of the current transgender ideology, which is permeating society at every level. I strongly recommend a good dose of a scientifically-based reality check to

---

[61] Ibid.
[62] https://www.pewresearch.org/science/2008/04/17/the-evidence-for-belief-an-interview-with-francis-collins/

anyone who denies basic, fundamental science and who derides believers in God as being uninformed and unintelligent. I would rather take Pascal's wager anytime than to waddle in the current miasma of subjectivism and relativism. I personally thank God every day for having created me and for having made me a child of His Church. I follow God and I rely on Nature which He created and which is scientifically observable. Hopefully, one day, the people who are in opposition to God and His science, will come to realize the beauty and reasonableness of His truth.

Chapter Eight

On Feminism, Education, Marriage, and Family

For this reason a man shall leave his father and his mother, and be joined to his wife; and they shall become one flesh. Genesis 2:24

The gradual decline in moral values and the loss of religious devotion has catapulted society, like never before, into embracing the actual cultural ideologies concerning everything sexual, from LGBTQ2S+ rights, abortion rights and transgender rights, to radical feminism, high divorce rates and the breakdown of families. Society has replaced God with ideological concepts. This leads inevitably to such actions as women refusing procreation via contraception and abortion, parents not being involved enough in their children's lives, social media taking over the education of children, adolescents grappling with anxiety and depression and men being caught in the middle of all this.

Regarding marriage and babies; if anybody still gets married nowadays, they do so with the viewpoint of not having children, preferring, for various reasons, to be childless. Given that the natural maternal and nurturing instinct is usually present in women, they will very often compensate for their childless status with a great deal of love and affection on domestic pets such as cats and dogs. I love animals, but when you think about it, raising cats and dogs will do nothing to help perpetuate humankind. Stephen White, executive director of The Catholic Project at The Catholic University of America and a fellow in Catholic Studies at the Ethics and Public Policy Center, discusses declining birth rates in his essay *Someone to dance with*,[1] in which he states the following: "*Birth rates are falling, not merely because of the economic pressures of policy decisions, but because would-be parents are no longer confident that raising children is a worthwhile endeavor. From a worldly perspective, they are simply deciding that kids are not worth the trouble and expense. Against a broader horizon - a transcendent, religious horizon - all of this changes... As man has lost a sense of transcendence, he has lost a proper appreciation for natural goods, too. It turns out that when we human beings turn our backs on God, all of creation - even that part of creation we call "human" - begins to fade into meaninglessness.*"[2] Given that God said to mankind to be fruitful (Genesis 1:28), mankind was supposed to reproduce itself in order to assure the survival of our species. The actual dearth of live births is leading us slowly, but surely, towards extinction if the tide is not stemmed, and turned, as soon as possible.

To begin, death comes in all kinds of ways, such as old age, disease, war, famine, accident, murder, abortion, natural calamity, death penalty, euthanasia and suicide. We therefore need to procreate at levels high enough to compensate for these human losses. According to *Our World in Data*,[3] the worldwide statistics on death

---

[1] https://www.theCatholicthing.org/2024/08/08/someone-to-dance-with/

[2] Ibid.

[3] https://ourworldindata.org/

for 2023 is 61 million people,[4] while the statistics on worldwide births for 2023 is 134 million babies.[5] By doing simple math, the world's population increased by 73 million people, which represents a net increase of 0.91%.[6] Based on yearly birth/death statistics and on population projections, the consensus is the following: "*As the number of births is expected to fall slowly and the number of deaths to rise, the global population growth rate will continue to fall. This is when the world population will stop increasing in the future.*"[7] Given that the actual population is aging, and more and more people are opting for childlessness, mainly through contraception, the future does not look too bright going forward. The American Psychological Association[8] discusses the subject of Americans wanting to live childless lives and quotes different findings: "*According to a February Pew Research Center Poll, 30% of 18-34-year-olds without kids aren't sure if they want children, and 18% say they don't want any.*[9] *That follows a rise between 2018 and 2021 in the percentage of non-parents under 50 who said they were "not too likely" or "not likely" to have kids.*"[10] This type of mindset is not surprising. When

---

[4] Hannah Ritchie and Edouard Mathieu (2023) - "How many people die and how many are born each year?" OurWorldInData.org. Retrieved from: 'https://ourworldindata.org/births-and-deaths' [Online Resource]

[5] Ibid.

[6] Ibid.

[7] Ibid.

[8] https://www.apa.org/monitor/2024/07/fewer-children#

[9] https://www.pewresearch.org/short-reads/2024/02/15/among-young-adults-without-children-men-are-more-likely-than-women-to-say-they-want-to-be-parents-someday/

[10] https://www.pewresearch.org/short-reads/2021/11/19/growing-share-of-childless-adults-in-u-s-dont-expect-to-ever-have-children/

you think about all the contracepting and aborting going on, and the push to codify abortion as a "right", it figures that less and less babies are being born.

The sexual revolution and the pro-feminist agendas that have been, and still are, being spearheaded and mandated, have exerted a major influence on the societal decline being seen, especially in the western hemisphere. The feminist movement began many decades ago, with the likes of Simone de Beauvoir, Margaret Sanger, Betty Friedan and Gloria Steinem, and others, influencing women everywhere to "stand up against the patriarchy" and "free themselves from their oppressors". While it is true that many women suffered at the hands of abusive men, they were not obliged to forgo their femininity, deny motherhood and destroy the traditional family unit altogether. I am not a feminist and I do believe that men are physically stronger than women and are supposed to care and protect women and children. Men who abuse women and children will have to answer to God eventually for their role in the radical feminism that has been unfolding since the mid-20th century. Radical feminism views women as being victims of men. When someone sincerely believes that they are a victim, they must destroy the enemy that is victimizing them in order to survive. The radical feminist therefore views the status of wife, mother and homemaker as victimhood. The oppressors, who are the cause of this victimhood, are therefore the patriarchs (husbands, fathers, clergy and colleagues) who must be eradicated. This mindset ultimately leads to the destruction of family life, mainly through the abandonment of motherhood, with women preferring to choose so-called self-fulfillment

Chapter Eight: On Feminism, Education, Marriage, and Family

over procreation. Women achieve this non-motherhood by the simple expedient of artificial contraception and abortion, euphemistically labeled as "reproductive health care" and "reproductive rights", which are deceptive terms given that there is no reproduction involved.

In his 1968 encyclical letter *Humanae Vitae*,[11] Pope Paul VI prophetically discussed the danger of men losing respect for women because of the prevalence of contraception: "*Another effect that gives cause for alarm is that a man who grows accustomed to the use of contraceptive methods may forget the reverence due to a woman, and, disregarding her physical and emotional equilibrium, reduce her to being a mere instrument for the satisfaction of his own desires, no longer considering her as his partner whom he should surround with care and affection.*"[12] This is exactly what we are seeing in our society half a century later. Men have become immune to women's emotions. They treat women as sexual objects. How can men respect women who deny their role as wife and mother, going so far as to kill their own baby, in their very own wombs? Even Pete Buttigieg, former U.S. Secretary of Transportation, had verbally stated, on July 31st 2024, that men have less responsibility thanks to abortion: "*Men are also more free in a country where we have a president [former president Joe Biden] who stands up for things like access to abortion care.*

---

[11] https://www.vatican.va/content/paul-vi/en/encyclicals/documents/hf_p-vi_enc_25071968_humanae-vitae.html
[12] Ibid.

Men are more free."¹³ A *Newsweek* article by Andrea Truddan, Vice-President of Heartbeat International, had this to say in response to Mr. Buttigieg's comment: "*Pete Buttigieg's recent comments about men being "more free" when women have access to abortion are deeply troubling. The remark reveals a perspective that not only undermines the inherent dignity and value of women, but also perpetuates a culture that allows men to evade responsibility and fail to support women in their time of need. This passing suggestion…implies that women's lives and choices are secondary to men's convenience…overlooks the profound effects - both physical and emotional - that abortion has on women. This view encourages a culture where men are absolved of their responsibilities…*"¹⁴ This is exactly what Pope Paul VI foresaw as the fallout from a contraceptive mentality, which is the basic denial of procreation.

I believe the root of the problem is that women envy men. They want what men have. They do not want to be beholden to men in any way, shape or form. They do not want to bear children despite engaging in sexual intercourse with men. And now, with the current social contagion of transgenderism, it's not good enough to mimic men. Women want to physically become men. Is it any wonder that humankind is on a slippery slope towards self-extinction?

---

¹³ https://www.Catholicnewsagency.com/news/258460/abortion-makes-men-more-free-pete-buttigieg-says

¹⁴ https://www.newsweek.com/pete-buttigieg-wrong-about-abortion-freedom-opinion-1933170

Chapter Eight: On Feminism, Education, Marriage, and Family 127

Women have the unique gift of bearing children. The survival of humankind depends on women throughout the world being mothers. According to statista.com, there have consistently been more men (males) than women (females) on earth, since the year 2000: *"Over the past 22 years, there were constantly more men than women living on the planet. Of the 7.95 billion people living on the earth in 2022, four billion were men and 3.95 billion were women. One fourth of the world's total population in 2022 were below 15 years."*[15] Imagine for a moment what the potential outcome would be if half of the sexually active women refused to procreate, preferring childlessness over raising children; there will ultimately be a lack of human beings needed to replace the dying populations.

There are many women out there who do want to get married and bear children, but do not because of overriding factors that make it well nigh impossible for them. Chief among them is not being able to find the right person. Surveys on the low marriage rates make a connection between the past and the present: *"There are just over six marriages for every 1,000 people in the United States, compared with a record 16.4 in 1946 after World War II, according to the Centers for Disease Control and Prevention's National Center for Health Statistics"*.[16] It would seem that life was simpler nearly a century ago. People had personal relationships; they spoke to each other face to face, instead of texting and scrolling interminably on their

---

[15] https://www.statista.com/statistics/1328107/global-population-gender/#

[16] https://www.Catholicnewsagency.com/news/258671/Catholic-women-discuss-the-challenges-of-modern-dating-culture

phones and relying on dating apps to do the socializing work for them. Nowadays, it's almost a miracle to engage in actual, face-to-face conversations with strangers. I remember a time when people would chat to each other on the city bus, to and from work; nowadays, every passenger is in their own bubble, endlessly scrolling on their smartphone, completely insulated from the people around them. Alone in a crowd, with no human interaction. I see this phenomenon everywhere. Even in social gatherings such as a dance hall for the 50+ crowd, men are on their phones instead of asking a woman to dance. What's the point of even going to a social event if you don't socialize? That's the whole point of these events: socializing!! In fact, that is exactly the way I met my husband: at a community dance event. If I, or he, had been in phone-scrolling mode, we would not be married today. Nothing beats good old-fashioned socializing!!

As regards families, given that the familial unit has changed over time, children do not have the traditional upbringing of times past. Adolescents are heavily influenced by school, their peers and social media. I have personally heard a mom tell her fourteen-year-old son to take charge of his own path as she was too busy taking care of her own existence. Her estranged husband, the boy's father, looked helplessly on as she was expounding on her rights of leading her own life and not wanting to have to deal with her son's school problems. I was personally flabbergasted at her rhetoric. I remember my own mother being wholeheartedly involved in everything that affected my life, including my education. There's nothing like knowing in your bones that your parent is committed to being a parent, in and

Chapter Eight: On Feminism, Education, Marriage, and Family 129

out of season. This abdication of parenting has an effect on a child. Children need structure and guidance. If they do not get it from their parents, they will subconsciously search for it elsewhere. Social media, political ideological currents, schools and peers will inevitably be their go-to guides. Many U.S. researchers have studied this shift in society: "*The Substance Abuse and Mental Health Services Administration conducted a … survey that analyzed the amount of counseling, medication, or other forms of mental health therapy minors underwent in 2023… 8.3 million youth ages 12 to 17 received mental health care…the results "were in line with the trend it's seen since 2009, namely, that "the percentage of teenagers who receive treatment for mental health has climbed practically every year.*"[17] Other reports make connections between fatherless children and mental health issues and behavior: "*In a report that compared dozens of studies conducted between 1987 and 2022, the America First Policy Institute (AFPI) found 'clear correlations between children raised in fatherless homes and developmental challenges ranging from bad grades, anxiety and suicide to violent behavior, drug use and criminality'.*"[18] In addition to the importance of a traditional familial entourage, the negative effects of social media have also been studied: "*Common Sense Media's study…urged that 'the negative effects of social media on young people's mental health is a top concern' … there are mounds*

---

[17] https://www.dailysignal.com/2024/08/13/8-3-million-minors-received-mental-care-in-2023-highlighting-a-decaying-culture/?

[18] https://washingtonstand.com/news/fathers-are-crucial-to-healthy-outcomes-for-kids-studies-confirm

of studies, as well as warnings from the U.S. Surgeon General, all putting a spotlight on the way social media is hurting teenagers."[19] These studies show the importance for parents to seriously take to heart their role as primary educators of their children. Parents must be ready to go above and beyond the supply of the basic physical needs, such as food and shelter, of their offspring. Teaching them the values of truth and reason, faith and scientific reality, tradition and discipline, as well as fostering confidence and sharing of ideas is essential to a healthy parent-child relationship. A child needs to be able to confide in his or her parents about issues, and be able to count on their solid, loving assistance, at all times, throughout their life. After all, being a parent is supposed to be a life-long commitment.

I wonder if today's parents are aware of what is going on in their children's lives. Do they know the extent to which their children are literally being groomed by Woke ideologues all over the country? I recommend that every parent makes a point of actively participating in the day-to-day existence of their children, encouraging conversations and discussions around the dinner table, from the very beginning of their offspring's lives, most especially when they begin their schooling years, from kindergarten onwards. Good structure, traditions, discipline, a good dose of moral values, and, dare I say it, religious values, can go a long way in helping to counter the gradual loss of their progeny to ideological cults, to social media and to mental illness. This is very important because there is a gradual erosion of parental rights being fostered in the education system. Minors are

---

[19] https://www.dailysignal.com/2024/08/13/8-3-million-minors-received-mental-care-in-2023-highlighting-a-decaying-culture/?

Chapter Eight: On Feminism, Education, Marriage, and Family 131

being aided by school authorities in taking life altering decisions without parental consent and/or parental knowledge. Children and teens are sometimes living a double life, mainly in connection with transgender issues such as preferred pronouns and preferred names, and even with medication use. Many students have medications at school that parents may not be aware of. School officials act as if they have the child's welfare at heart more than the parents do. This should not be the case. Parents are the people who should, and usually do, have the very best interests of their children at heart.

A recent example of the exclusion of parents is at the heart of an August 2024 case in the United States, in Denver, Colorado. Since 2021, there is a school district policy called the Parental Exclusion Policy which prevents schools from notifying parents about their child's transitioning if the student in question does not consent.[20] A counselor at Brighton High School was relying on this policy when she was enabling a fourteen-year-old female student to secretly transition to the opposite sex without her parents' knowledge and consent. Life-altering treatments such as breast removal surgery and hormone treatments were recommended by the transgender therapist with whom the young girl had been referred to, by the school counselor. The parents were never notified of these momentous events in their child's life. The girl in question eventually regretted the "transition". The parents and their daughter have filed a complaint and are suing the school, hoping to combat the policies that

---

[20] https://www.ncregister.com/cna/parents-sue-colorado-school-for-secretly-facilitating-daughter-s-gender-transition

enabled the school to keep this crucial information from them: "'*Social transitioning is a powerful form of psychological treatment*', the complaint notes, arguing that in minors '*may only be done under the watchful supervision of a trained mental health professional and with close parental involvement at every step of the way*'."[21] It is imperative for parents everywhere to always stand up for their parental rights and for the health and safety of their children.

Parents need to be aware of how the education system is advancing the current Woke ideology in schools; not only in high school, but at the elementary level as well. The very nature of education is supposed to be the search for truth; teachers are called to enlighten the truth and students are supposed to search for the truth by thinking, growing, developing and asking questions in order to get to the truth, instead of being told what to think, which is, in effect, indoctrination. This, in turn, propagates changing society through activism instead of understanding reality: this is basically what the so-called critical theory is all about. What is currently being subtly propagated in classes is more of an indoctrination in Woke ideology than a search for objective truth. Noelle Mering, author of *Awake, Not Woke: A Christian Response to the Cult of Progressive Ideology* (Tan Books, 2021) and fellow at the Ethics and Public Policy Centre, explains this issue in the series *In Focus*: *Confronting a Woke World* (Faith and Reason Website): "Traditionally, you would say 'You study and you learn and are educated, for the sake of coming to truth.

---

[21] Ibid.

Chapter Eight: On Feminism, Education, Marriage, and Family 133

If you are wrong, you want to be corrected, so you want to invite debate, you want to invite dialogue, because your goal is truth. If your goal is not truth, but power, you want to silence dissent, you don't want to invite it.'... The goal (of critical theory) is not to grapple and wrestle with reality, in order to receive it, but to change it. You have to change reality. So, becoming an activist becomes part of your education, under critical theory. You're not just supposed to think, you're actually supposed to go out and change the world, for the sake of the ideology, to raise consciousness...this is part of Marxism...it's a false consciousness."[22] I strongly recommend viewing this series; Noelle Mering discusses this ideology which is taking hold of society and, more importantly, taking hold of our children, with her host, Fr. Dave Pivonka, Franciscan President of the University of Steubenville. Perhaps this series will help parents have an open discussion of their own, with their children, in order to make them aware of how they are being manipulated by society.

Another huge factor that is affecting society is the change in language regarding marriage and families, among other things. For millennia, the word "marriage" has always been crystal clear, and understood the world over, as being the recognized legal and/or religious union of one man and one woman, while "family" has always been recognized as mother, father and the offspring which is issued forth from the procreative union of man and wife. Thousands of years of this accepted traditional reality of marriage and family has been completely turned on its head in the space of a few decades.

---

[22] https://faithandreason.com/episodes/key-thinkers/

With the advent of same-sex unions wanting to be universally recognized as marriage, the language has forever been altered. What was a given reality yesterday has become a linguistic "reality" today. So we now have "gay marriage". The logical next steps came very soon. Families with two fathers or two mothers are affirmed as a family and transgender "families" are being celebrated. I once met a lesbian couple who both decided to transition to the opposite sex. They are now two "men" who have adopted a little boy and are part of the lauded "rainbow families" in our community. The issue with language is that words do matter. We need a common language in order to live in harmony.[23] When the meaning of words are changed by activists and ideologues, generations of people will not agree, according to their reason and established definitions. If someone tells me, for example, they met a family at the park, I should be permitted to assume that they are talking about a "traditional" family: a biological female (mother) and a biological male (father) with a child or children. How can I be expected to think that they are talking about a transgender "family"? The non-traditional families are imposing their lifestyle choices on society, demanding affirmation by changing norms and language, thus creating confusion. We are constantly having to weigh our words in order not to "offend" anyone. Innocuous words such as "he" and "she" have become weaponized, going so far as to cost people their jobs and livelihoods. This is so entrenched in our current culture that there is now a bill in Massachusetts that wants to eliminate the words "mother" and "father" from parental rights: *"Among its provisions, the bill, ... removes the*

---

[23] https://faithandreason.com/episodes/do-you-hate-me/

words "mother" and "father" from Massachusetts' parental recognition laws. Gov. Maura Healey, who described Massachusetts as "proud to be a national leader and trailblazer when it comes to LGBTQ+ equality" promised to sign the bill into law."[24] As Charles J. Russo, Research Professor of Law and Chair of Education at the University of Dayton, Ohio, as well as Adjunct Professor at Notre Dame University of Australia states on this issue: *"The bill's... provision seeks to alter family structures that have existed since the beginning of time by dropping the word "father" and replacing "mother of the child" with "person who gave birth"... It seems evident that Massachusetts' elected officials have taken aim at Christian and traditional beliefs, and related values..."*[25] As Prof. Russo further explains: *"...people of faith were denied opportunities to adopt and/or serve as foster parents while others lost custody of their minor child who sought to transition because their religious values prevented them from supporting the LGBTQ agenda. Further, believers are challenging a state law in California that trammels parental rights by banning public school officials from informing them when their young seek to change their pronouns and/or sexes without their approval.*[26] It is quite ironic that the ideologues who spout "diversity" and "inclusivity" in every speech they make on this subject are the very same people who do not include the traditional section of the population; are we not also part of the diversity landscape? Why is our point of view not being

---

[24] https://www.Catholicworldreport.com/2024/08/06/massachusetts-bill-will-eliminate-mother-and-father-from-parenting-laws/
[25] Ibid.
[26] Ibid.

included? *Au contraire*, we are being summarily dismissed and being railroaded into accepting, affirming and taking part in the ideological viewpoint. In this particular bill, the elected officials are downright excluding mothers and fathers by removing their appellations from the official records. They are not being recognized for who they are. I see this as a total rejection of who we are as a traditional people. What happened to the banner cry of "accept me for who I am" that is the overriding theme of the LGBTQ agenda? Why can't this phrase not be said by anyone other than an LGBTQ person? Mothers and fathers are obviously not being accepted, or recognized, for who they are: biological males and females who procreated a child and who are caring for every aspect of this child's life. Even more so if you happen to be a believing Christian family, whose perfect role model is the Holy Family of Mary, Joseph and Jesus, the familial unit *par excellence*. By rejecting the traditional family unit, are they not implicitly rejecting the Holy Family? Are they not rejecting God's vision of the family, such as described in the Book of Genesis, when God gave Eve to Adam, and told them to be fruitful?

Finally, while radical feminism and societal norms and ideologies are waging an assault on traditional marriage and family, we must also take into account the behaviors of men and women towards each other. Being married implies complete fidelity to one another. I simply cannot understand spouses who accept infidelity as part of their union. I have heard of wives overlooking their husband's indiscretions and husbands accepting their wives' infidelity for the sake of convenience or for financial reasons. I am quite opposed to this mindset; no "mutual understanding" for my marriage.

Chapter Eight: On Feminism, Education, Marriage, and Family

It's complete fidelity or nothing. That's the way it should be. It is explicitly woven in our marriage vows; the part about forsaking all others. In addition to faithfulness, I believe that spouses are meant to be helpmates. I personally believe that both husbands and wives have a duty to advise their spouse and, dare I say it, "tell" them what to do, in certain instances. For example, I would much prefer my husband tell me outright that he doesn't want me to walk around sporting a micro-skirt than to keep his mouth shut under the pretext that I am not his child and can do what I want. Frankly, such *laissez-faire* smacks of lack of caring. Spouses are meant to help each other out. It goes without saying that each person makes their own choices/decisions, but at least the attempt to steer one in the right direction should be attempted. Husbands nowadays are scared stiff to voice an opinion, due largely in part to male-bashing feminist rhetoric. Same thing for wives; they do not want to be regarded as henpeckers. How many wives have kept silent in the face of their husbands spending time and money on pornography instead of speaking up from the get-go? What business does a husband have (or anyone else for that matter), to be hooked on porn when he has a wife and family to take care of? What business does a wife have of going "for a coffee" with a male colleague, after work? Why would a husband go have lunch with a female neighbor without his wife? Why would a wife go to a party with someone other than her husband? However innocent all of these scenarios might be, is it not plausible that there is more to it than meets the eye? How many times have we heard the easy explanation "It just happened; it wasn't planned" when a spouse finds out that the other cheated? Nothing "just happens". There is always a first step which leads to the inevitable. All this to say that finding a suitable person to share one's life with, in marriage, and caring for each other, for life, is a traditional mainstay that needs to be fostered and protected, most especially when it comes to the begetting and rearing of children, who are, after all is said and done, our future.

Chapter Nine

On Catholicism and Freedom of Religion

"Everything is from God, who has reconciled us to himself through Christ and gave us the ministry of reconciliation. ... Therefore we are ambassadors for Christ, since God is making his appeal through us. We plead on Christ's behalf, 'Be reconciled to God'" (2 Cor. 5:18, 20)

Religion has been around, in one form or another, for thousands of years. Greek mythology abounds with gods and deities. The Old Testament prophets announced the advent of a Messiah, thus preparing the way for the New Testament Gospels. Belief in one Almighty God was firmly established with Judaism and Christianity. The third monotheistic religion is Islam, when the prophet Muhammad was visited by Jibril, the angel of God, in 610 A.D. and the word of Allah (God) was shared via the Qur'an. According to statista.com, these three religions account for roughly 55% of the world's population.[1] Other religions, such as Buddhism, Hinduism and countless others, clearly reflect the need for religiosity and spirituality in most people's lives. Even self-professed atheists and agnostics need something to believe in, be it humanism or environmentalism or any other ism they can cling to. It is part and parcel of mankind to be spiritual or religious, in some guise or other. As a Catholic myself, I firmly believe in one God: the Holy Trinity, God the Father, God the Son (Our Lord and Savior Jesus Christ), and God the Holy Spirit. I

---

[1] https://www.statista.com/statistics/374704/share-of-global-population-by-religion/

believe everything that the Holy Catholic Church teaches and believes because it is God who revealed it, through His only begotten Son, Jesus Christ.

Living in a democracy means that I should have the freedom of religion and freedom of speech, which enables me to proclaim my faith without fear of persecution. While religious liberty concerns immunity from coercion in civil society and does not imply all religions are equally true, freedom of religion is for every religion, everywhere, and it must be allowed to be exercised within the just public order and common good (*Dignitatis Humanae* 2, 7). However, we do not live in a perfect world. There is only one perfect place, and that place is Eternal Life with God, usually called Heaven. Until we, hopefully, get to Heaven, life on earth is a constant struggle, one of which is a lack of complete freedom to fearlessly and publicly exercise one's religion.

Many countries in the world are downright persecuting people on the basis of their religious beliefs. China has a very bad track record of human rights abuses and persecution of religious minorities. We are all aware of China's persecution of Tibetan monks: "*Tibetan Buddhism is seen as a threat to the occupying Chinese state and is tightly regulated, with Chinese officials closely monitoring and controlling religious activity at monasteries and nunneries.*"[2] The current Dalai Lama, the spiritual guide of Buddhists, has been living in exile

---

[2] https://freetibet.org/freedom-for-tibet/occupation-of-tibet/

since 1959,³ separated from his people. There are also the Uygher Muslims who are being detained in concentration camps in China and are being denied their freedom of worshiping God according to their religious precepts: *"The Chinese government closely monitors Uyghur religious institutions. Even ordinary acts such as praying or going to a mosque may be a basis for arrest or detention."*⁴ The underground Catholics in China are also paying the price for merely trying to practice their spiritual convictions.⁵ Countries such as Saudi Arabia,⁶ Iran,⁷ and North Korea⁸ are curtailing the Christian religion, and Nigeria⁹ is absolutely persecuting Christians, as evidenced by Boko Haram kidnapping whole communities of Catholics on a regular basis.¹⁰ Nicaragua¹¹ is another country that is fiercely dismantling the Catholic religion; President Daniel Ortega is systematically arresting priests and bishops, imprisoning them

---

    ³   https://www.theguardian.com/world/2021/jul/31/tibet-and-china-clash-over-next-reincarnation-of-the-dalai-lama
    ⁴   https://www.ushmm.org/genocide-prevention/countries/china/chinese-persecution-of-the-uyghurs
    ⁵   https://international.la-croix.com/religion/we-cannot-leave-the-church-in-china-under-the-control-of-a-party-that-destroys-everything
    ⁶   https://globalchristianrelief.org/christian-persecution/countries/saudi-arabia/
    ⁷ https://www.stefanus-usa.org/news/persecution-of-christians-intensifies-in-iran#:
    ⁸   https://globalchristianrelief.org/christian-persecution/countries/north-korea/
    ⁹   https://adfinternational.org/commentary/nigeria-most-dangerous-country-christians#:
    ¹⁰   https://www.genocidewatch.com/single-post/nigeria-s-silent-slaughter-62-000-christians-murdered-since-2000#
    ¹¹ https://www.uscirf.gov/countries/nicaragua

and/or sending them away in exile and banning public expression of religious worship.[12] In fact, the Catholic faith is often being harassed, denied, demeaned and desecrated throughout the world.[13]

Another recent example of Christian persecution is the case of Abdulbaqi Saeed Abdo, a Yemeni husband and father of five, who converted from Islam to Christianity: "*Abdo was arrested by Egyptian authorities in 2021 for his involvement with a Facebook page that is dedicated to supporting people who have converted from Islam to Christianity. He was living as a UNHCR registered asylum seeker in Egypt following the death threats he received in his home country of Yemen after he converted to Christianity.*"[14] This man essentially does not have the basic human right of freedom of religion, nor freedom of speech. He is not free to even explain Christian theology. After spending more than two years in prison, he has decided to embark on a hunger strike, which he explains in a heart wrenching letter to his wife and children: "*My beloved wife and children, who are precious to my heart and soul. …I started today on the 7 of August 2024 a partial strike…. And the reason of my strike* (is that) *that they arrested me without any legal justification. They did not convict me for any violation of the law. And they did not set me free during my remand imprisonment which was ended 8 months ago.*"[15] The lack of religious tolerance which is being meted out for anyone who dares

---

[12] https://www.state.gov/reports/2022-report-on-international-religious-freedom/nicaragua/

[13] https://globalchristianrelief.org/christian-persecution/countries/

[14] https://adfinternational.org/news/father-imprisoned-egypt

[15] Ibid.

Chapter Nine: On Catholicism and Freedom of Religion

convert to the Christian faith is totally unacceptable, especially given the fact that when Christians convert to Islam, neither the Christian Church, nor the secular government, violate those converts in the least. Should there not be at least some semblance of reciprocal respect? As Kelsey Zorzi, ADF (Alliance for the Defense of Freedom) International's Director of Advocacy for Global Religious Freedom stated: *"The gross human rights violations and injustice perpetrated by the Egyptian authorities in this case are clear and expose how the laws in Egypt are being abused to punish those with minority views and beliefs. Governments across the world are failing to uphold appropriate legal standards for freedom of religion and speech, allowing rampant criminalisation of social media posts and religious practice to go unchecked. Whether in the Middle East, Europe or elsewhere, we must urgently do better to protect basic human rights, and allow each individual to freely hold and express their own beliefs."*[16] Once again, people everywhere should stand up for freedom of religion; when freedom to exercise one's religious beliefs is taken away, every other freedom is at risk, for every single person, not just in other countries, but in our own Western Civilisation.

Another example is in the sports realm; the advocacy group Coptic Solidarity is calling for an official investigation into the IOC (International Olympic Committee) for the apparent discrimination of Egyptian Coptic Christian athletes. In Egypt's 154 athletes present at the summer Olympic games in 2024, only one single athlete was

---

[16] https://adfinternational.org/news/father-imprisoned-egypt

Chrisitan.[17] According to Samuel Tadros, advisor to the Philos Project,[18] a Christian Advocacy in the Near-East, Christians have been historically discriminated against in Egypt and the Copts represent half of the Christian population in Egypt.[19] They are now claiming that Coptic soccer players are being discriminated against by Egypt and have a website featuring their allegations and the accompanying petition.[20] They are calling on the Egyptian Minister of Youth and Sport, the president of FIFA (International Federation of Football Associations) and the president of the Confederation of African Football "*to open an investigation and work to end all the sectarian discrimination against Coptic Christians in the Egyptian soccer clubs*".[21] Again, it is mandatory for Christians to stand up for their right to exist and be recognized for who they are and for what they believe. Each and every time I encounter some form of discrimination against the Christian population, I cannot help but notice how "the other side" clamors for tolerance, acceptance, affirmation and recognition of their "rights" (i.e. abortion rights, LGBTQ rights, gay rights, euthanasia rights, transgender rights, and on and on), but when it comes to Christian rights (i.e. freedom of religion, expressing publicly one's beliefs, talking about God and religion, etc...), there is absolutely no tolerance, acceptance, affirmation or recognition. Talk about one-sidedness and

---

[17] EWTN News Nightly; Aug 16, 2024; https://www.youtube.com/watch?v=IakJ9TyV-uM

[18] https://philosproject.org/

[19] Ibid.

[20] https://www.letcoptsplay.org/

[21] Ibid.

Chapter Nine: On Catholicism and Freedom of Religion

non-reciprocity. Society seems pre-conditioned to shut down and cancel Christians at every possible opportunity, including sports!

Even in our own continent of North America, there is some kind of Catholic/Christian ill treatment which exists, albeit on a much milder scale than the killings, torture and imprisonment going on overseas. Oftentimes, intolerance of religiosity is demonstrated by a show of disrespect and/or ridicule that is aimed at anyone who believes in God. One just has to look at the opening ceremony for the Paris 2024 Olympics on July 26th, 2024, which caused a major uproar due to the disrespectful portrayal, by Drag Queens, of the Last Supper, which is Christianity's most sacred and deeply held belief: the institution of the Eucharist.[22] This parody sparked outrage throughout the world; even Muslim leaders condemned this disrespectful act.[23] Not only is this type of dismissive behavior coming from society at large and from the media, but also from within our own family circles, colleagues, friends and acquaintances.

Being ridiculed for believing in God is the height of dismissiveness. I have personally experienced this many times. A particular episode comes to mind. About eight years ago, I was referred to a specialist for my "trigger thumb", a condition affecting my right hand and thumb, due to a swollen flexor tendon. I kept having clicks and pops every time I had to extend my thumb. I had been afflicted

---

[22] https://bcCatholic.ca/news/canada/olympic-organizers-abused-their-position-in-last-supper-mockery-Catholic-civil-rights-league-says
[23] https://www.Catholicnewsagency.com/news/258450/muslim-leaders-condemn-disgraceful-olympics-scene-it-offended-us-as-much-as-them

with this painful condition for many months, trying every remedy imaginable to relieve it. My family doctor was stumped as well, opting to refer me to an orthopedic specialist. On the very first visit, within five minutes of being in this doctor's office, he was attempting to influence me to let him cut open the base of my thumb in order to do a "routine" surgery, then and there, in his office. Whoa!!! I absolutely recoiled at the swiftness of his diagnosis and treatment plan. I politely refused, saying that I wanted to think about it and research my options. He went on to paint a very bleak picture of my condition getting worse over time and that only a surgical intervention could alleviate the symptoms. At this point, I calmly told him that I was a believer and would pray on it, before taking a final decision. His response was to laugh out loud and ask me loudly, in a derisive tone of voice, "What does religion have to do with it?" He did not show respect for me as a patient, nor as a believer. I obviously never returned to this particular doctor. His utter lack of tolerance was appalling, to say nothing of his lack of professionalism. I never lodged a complaint for the simple reason that I didn't think it would have been given any credence since it would have been religious-based. After all, my experience of society is that it is quite secular in its perspective and tends to dismiss believers as not worthy of due respect. As it turns out, one of my kindergarten students at the time had noticed that I had a problem with my thumb; she sweetly told me that she would pray for me. I kid you not, my thumb completely healed naturally, just like that, even to this day!! I've often heard that God listens to the sincere prayers of children and mothers. All I can say is, that on this particular occasion, a child prayed for me and my

Chapter Nine: On Catholicism and Freedom of Religion

thumb was healed. Coincidence? No one can tell with absolute certainty; therefore, who are we to cast aspersions on the sincere religious beliefs of others? Imagine for a moment if this little girl had voiced her prayerful intention in front of this medical specialist; his derisive lack of respect might have rendered her incapable of ever expressing her belief again. No one has the right to destroy something as fundamental as one's belief in God; it goes against decency and goodwill.

The lack of tolerance for one's belief in God is ubiquitous. It plays out in the public sphere on a daily basis. Sometimes, it reaches to the very echelons of laws and politics. One blatant disregard of religious beliefs is the overriding of conscience rights of Catholic medical doctors, in Catholic hospitals throughout North America. As Catholics, these doctors truly believe that abortion, the killing of an innocent, defenseless human being, is morally wrong; they object and refuse to perform an abortion, which is explicitly forbidden under Catholic doctrine. This being said, governments are dismissing these religious and conscientious objectors. Doctors and nurses, in Catholic hospitals, are being harassed to perform abortions, which are termed as "emergency health care" and "essential reproductive health care" and just plain "health care". The United States Conference of Catholic Bishops explains the situation: "*For decades they have attempted to force Catholic hospitals to provide abortions or go out of business… the campaign to deny Catholic health care providers their rights of conscience has met with some success… Today, abortion rights activists are implementing a subtle and incremental strategy to undo conscience rights...Abortion activists have also enlisted the support of state and local governments in discriminating against pro-life health care providers...Defending such rights is not just a Catholic issue. It is a fundamental human right to refuse to take part in morally evil actions..."*[24] If medical doctors and nurses are publicly having their beliefs summarily dismissed, imagine how "regular folks" can be discriminated against because of their faith, in their daily routines at work, with their colleagues and at home, with their own family members, friends and acquaintances.

My own extended family is very large; innumerable in-laws who, for the most part, are non-believers. Very few of them respect my beliefs. Their reactions run the gamut of outright hostility and name-calling, to pitying guffaws at my "naïveté" in reading the bible or following the teachings of the Catholic Church. One in-law went so far as to chastise my spouse because he went to Sunday Mass; she evinced utter incredulity that he would take part in such a futile practice. Her exclamation of "What!? WHY!?" was a sight to behold. Another member of the family pontificated on how it was wrong of Jesus to choose only men as apostles. I have heard people in my entourage advocate for childhood masturbation, and then declare that they, the masturbating young, are pure and innocent and do not need to go to confession. Then there was my wedding ceremony, where a few of the invited guests were actually taking selfies during the consecration, the very holiest part of Mass, as evidenced by the pictures in my wedding album. If I dare try to elucidate certain

---

[24] https://www.usccb.org/committees/pro-life-activities/assault-Catholic-health-care

Chapter Nine: On Catholicism and Freedom of Religion

teachings of the Church, I am branded a fanatic and told that nobody wants to hear what I am saying. I hope God will forgive me for having decided to never speak about religion and morals to these people ever again. I have promised myself to keep my mouth shut and try to block out the irreverent comments I hear. A very good friend of mine told me that I will speak just as loudly by mere examples of patience and kindness; in simpler terms, actions speak louder than words. Time will tell. In the meantime, I am keeping a close eye on whatever freedom of religion we still have in Canada and am empathizing wholeheartedly with my persecuted Christian brothers and sisters worldwide.

Chapter Ten

On Arts and Artists

"He's filled him with the Spirit of God, with skill, ability, and know-how for making all sorts of things, to design and work in gold, silver, and bronze; to carve stones and set them; to carve wood, working in every kind of skilled craft." Exodus 35: 30-35

I love watching movies. I enjoy listening to good music. I admire beautiful paintings. There's nothing like reading a good book on a rainy afternoon. All of these joys are made possible due to talented and gifted artists. In fact, some of the greatest artistic talents, universally recognized and lauded throughout history have been Catholics. Are readers and moviegoers aware that the author of *The Lord of the Rings,* J.R.R. Tolkien, was a devout Catholic? As is actor/director Mel Gibson; his masterpiece, 2004's *The Passion of the Christ*, is simply breathtaking. As for painters and sculptors, one just has to mention Michealangelo's Sistine Chapel ceiling or his Statue of David, Leonardo Da Vinci' Last Supper or his Mona Lisa, Bernini's Baldaquino in St.Peter's Basilica in Rome and Caravaggio's techniques in combining lights and shadows in his famous painting of *The Calling of Saint Matthew*, to evince sheer admiration for their wondrous talents and gifts. These are just a drop in the ocean of famous Catholic artists and the contributions they gave the world. And it is abundantly clear that the Catholic Church is, and has been, a patron of the arts, since the very beginning of Christendom.

Saint Luke, one of the Gospel writers, is credited with the famous icon of the Virgin Mary with the child Jesus: *"For iconographers, St. Luke is revered as the first (according to tradition) to write an icon of the Blessed Mother. In iconography, the verb "to write" is used rather than "to paint," as an icon is considered visual theology."*[1] Furthermore, *"There are a number of images of Mary found on cave walls in Egypt, where hermits decorated their cells with holy images, and there seem to be images of her on the walls of the Roman catacombs."*[2] Art itself is a way of expressing truth and beauty. In fact, Dr. Jem Sullivan, an associate professor in Catechetics in the School of Theology and Religious Studies at the Catholic University of America, in Washington, D.C., is very eloquent about the expression of truth and beauty in art, as an educational tool in the teaching of the Catholic faith: *"Her research and publications focus on liturgical catechesis and the place of beauty and the arts in catechesis and evangelization."*[3] Just gazing on beautiful artwork can enkindle a love of the sacred in even the most hardened heart. The same can be said of a song or melody.

One of the instances I enjoy listening to music is when I sometimes take the city bus to go downtown for appointments. I like watching the scenery go by, with my headphones on and listening to songs. Have you ever listened to Jackie Evancho's rendition of the

---

[1] https://www.wordonfire.org/articles/saint-luke-the-artist/#

[2] https://www.redlandsdailyfacts.com/2011/06/17/legend-of-st-lukes-portrait-of-mary/

[3] https://trs.Catholic.edu/faculty-and-research/faculty-profiles/sullivan-jem/index.html

Chapter Ten: On Arts and Artists

Lord's Prayer (the *Our Father*)? I get goosebumps every time I hear it. As musician, author, composer and producer David Foster[4] said: *"I think this is one of the most beautifully constructed melodies ever, in the history of music. It's one of my favorites..."*[5] In fact, many prayers have been put to music by talented composers and musicians, past and present. Gounod and Shubert's versions of the Ave Maria, Handel's Messiah and Mozart's Ave Verum Corpus, among others, are perfect examples of artistic talent being used to highlight the beauty of Christianity.

On the flip side, however, there are some artists who use their talents in order to desecrate or undermine the Christian faith, while others, who create good depictions of Christianity, unfortunately use it to perform un-Christian acts. I am referring here to the Catholic Mosaicist Artist, Father Marco Rupnik, a recognized mosaïc artist whose artwork is featured in churches, chapels, shrines and sanctuaries all over the world. Such places as the Lourdes Grotto in France, where the Virgin Mary is believed to have appeared to Saint Bernadette Soubirous in 1858, and the Vatican, have showcased his artwork in full regalia, for all to gaze upon. For those not familiar with this particular case, it is credibly alleged that the former Jesuit priest had been abusing women religious for decades, psychologically, sexually, and spiritually, going so far as to incorporate sacred liturgy and sacred art in the acts of abuse.[6] If this is indeed true, and

---

[4] https://davidfoster.com/
[5] https://www.youtube.com/watch?v=Vg2AsS4CErM
[6] https://www.Catholicnewsagency.com/news/258311/take-down-his-art-or-not-who-is-alleged-serial-abuser-father-marko-rupnik

all evidence points to the veracity of these claims, what he has done is downright sacrilegious. He has been expelled by his Jesuit order and is being investigated by the Vatican. But what is very disturbing in this case is the fact that his artwork is still being displayed in major venues across the globe. So far, the Knights of Columbus, in America, have taken the decision and the necessary steps of covering up the mosaics which were displayed on the walls of the Saint John Paul II National Shrine in Washington, D.C.[7] There is also the Bishop of Lourdes who has decreed, in March 2025, that Rupnik's artwork be covered at the Lourdes Grotto.[8] Many critics argue about separating an artist from his art. For example, the great artist Caravaggio was involved in murder and other unsavory incidents and his art is prominently displayed and revered to this day. What is different in the particular case of Marco Rupnik is the undeniable fact that he is a priest. Caravaggio was not a priest. Think what you will, but as far as I am concerned, a priest has a higher mandate of Christian responsibility than the average mortal, by the mere fact of the sacred vows he undertook in becoming a priest, such as the vow of chastity and his priestly duty of leading his flock to God and Heaven, (just like Saint John Marie Vianney (1786-1859), the holy Curé of Ars[9] whose life is a lesson to priests everywhere). Caravaggio was a poor sinner, just like the rest of humanity. While Fr. Rupnik is also a poor sinner, his sin is compounded by the betrayal of his priestly vows

---

[7] https://www.kofc.org/en/resources/communications/kofc-announces-conclusion-of-mosaic-review-process.pdf

[8] https://www.lepelerin.com/religions-et-spiritualites/lactualite-de-leglise/lourdes-camoufle-les-mosaiques-de-rupnik-11497

[9] https://www.olrl.org/lives/vianney.shtml

and the distortion of his priestly powers of influencing his flock. The faithful under his priestly care have been betrayed. A priest is supposed to be a Christ-like figure. The crimes he is alleged to have committed are far from being Christ-like. Every time one sees his artwork, one is immediately brought face-to-face with his alleged crimes. So far, in August of the year 2024, he is still walking around free, exercising his artistic métier, as if nothing out of the ordinary is going on. This is a very difficult case; it will perhaps take a very long time for the Church and the law to decide what should be done with this man's artistic representations and with the man himself.

Father Rupnik aside, there are modern artists working in the field of sculptures and paintings who are not priests, but lay people, who use their art in a sacrilegious manner, while justifying their portrayals as being something praiseworthy. Such examples as the 1987 "urine" Christ photograph by artist Andres Serrano raised quite an uproar at the time. While this man is not a priest, he nevertheless is called to respect the sacred and use his talents for the purpose of edification through beauty. In my view, and many others' view, portraying our Lord and Savior Jesus Christ soaking in a jar of the artist's own urine is not the height of sacred beauty and respect for our crucified God who gave his life for humanity. I am not a professional artistic critic, so I would not presume to attempt an artistic critique of this man's artwork. As a Catholic however, I prefer to gaze on a regular crucifix and ponder the wondrous sacrifice of Jesus dying on a cross for love of us and for the salvation of sinners everywhere. We all know that Jesus was extremely ill-treated; we do not need to see him submerged in urine to understand his persecution.

Another modern-day artist who has crossed the line of decency is Austrian sculptor Esther Straub. She has depicted the Blessed Virgin Mary, legs wide open, giving birth, with a full frontal view of the head of Jesus emerging from her birth canal, hence the name of *The Crowning* for this sculpture. This is actually a pun, given that the Catholic understanding of "the crowning" is in relation to Mary being crowned Queen of Heaven (the Coronation (Crowning) of Mary is contemplated in the fifth decade of the rosary in the Glorious Mysteries of the Rosary)[10]. A few days after the statue was put on display in the Austrian Cathedral of Linz, of all places, it was decapitated by an unknown person. Frankly, these types of so-called religious depictions are exercises in bad taste, to say the least. German Cardinal Gerhardt Müller described it as: *"advertising for feminist ideology that violates the natural sense of modesty."*[11] He is actually on the mark in his opinion. According to the Hyperallergic website, an online publication in contemporary perspectives on art, culture and more: *"The artist stated that she had developed the sculpture to "address the gap in the birth of Christ from a feminist perspective," pointing to the sanitized depictions of infant Jesus in the manger. "Most images of the Virgin Mary were made by men and have therefore often served patriarchal interests," she noted."*[12] When the

---

[10] https://marian.org/mary/rosary/glorious-mysteries

[11] https://www.Catholicnewsagency.com/news/258233/cardinal-muller-condemns-statue-of-virgin-mary-giving-birth-displayed-in-austrian-cathedral

[12] https://hyperallergic.com/931419/sculpture-of-virgin-mary-in-labor-beheaded-in-austrian-cathedral/

Chapter Ten: On Arts and Artists

statue was first exhibited, before the beheading, a petition for its removal was circulated, arguing that *"the birth of Christ is one of the central mysteries of the Christian faith" and that artists have intentionally avoided depicting Mary in labor for the last 2,000 years."*[13] Indeed, these protestors believed that art should teach the faith through beauty and not through feminist ideals of reinventing two thousand years of Gospel revelation. The birth of Christ has always been viewed as a sacred mystery and venerated as such. Who are we to break so-called barriers in the divine revelation of his Incarnation? Throughout history, the world's greatest artists have treated this subject with the utmost sublime reverence to the Blessed Virgin Mary, and that is the way it should be. In fact, the birth of any child should be viewed as a great gift to be beheld with modest admiration. I am personally not interested in seeing explicit anatomical depictions of Jesus coming into the world. His mere presence is sufficient unto itself.

Finally, it is my conviction that artists, be they painters, writers, actors, directors, writers, sculptors, composers, musicians, singers or any other purveyor of artistic expression, should treat depictions of religiosity with respect and reverence, just as every other category of isms demand respect and reverence for their personal belief system, including LGBTQ lobbyists and Pro-Choicers and Atheists and everyone in between. If I watch a movie about Jesus, I don't appreciate seeing him depicted as a regular man with regular failings and temptations. I want to see a Gospel-based portrayal of him, as the Son of God who came for our ultimate salvation. Apart from a few

---

[13] Ibid.

deviances, this is mainly what has been the norm in the artistic world, which has deeply and significantly enriched mankind with their portrayals for many centuries. I hope that the next generations of artists follow in the footsteps of the Great Masters and bring truth and beauty to people everywhere.

Chapter Eleven

On Euthanasia and Assisted Suicide and On Death and Suffering

"No one is master of the breath of life so as to retain it, and none has mastery of the day of death." – Ecclesiastes 8:8

"Those who shut their ears to the cry of the poor will themselves call out and not be answered." – Proverbs 21:13

"Do not cast me aside in my old age; as my strength fails, do not forsake me." – Psalm 71:9

"Bear one another's burdens, and so you will fulfill the law of Christ." – Galatians 6:2

"Consider it all joy, my brothers, when you encounter various trials, for you know that the testing of your faith produces perseverance." – James 1:2-3

"But rejoice to the extent that you share in the sufferings of Christ, so that when his glory is revealed you may also rejoice exultantly." – 1 Peter 4:13

"The God of all grace who called you to his eternal glory through Christ [Jesus] will himself restore, confirm, strengthen, and establish you after you have suffered a little." – 1 Peter 5:10

Modern society has, for the most part, embraced the notion that all that matters is one's personal happiness and how one should not be impeded in one's pursuit of it. Suffering must be avoided at all costs, to the point where euthanasia and assisted suicide are becoming enshrined in law, in more and more countries across the Western hemisphere. Many persons in my own entourage publicly proclaim how they want "a needle in the arm" to end their life as soon as the pain and suffering makes itself felt; that's all. "What's the point of suffering?" is the common rhetorical question I hear all the time. But is this really the way to go? Killing everyone off at their request? I personally do not think this is the way to view death and suffering. I accept the way of the cross which Jesus Christ went through. I do not want to suffer, but if and when I do, as we are pretty much all destined to do, for one reason or another, I want to unite my sufferings with His sufferings. I believe in redemptive suffering and in its value of atoning for my sins and hopefully diminish my time in purgatory. Have you ever heard the phrase "Offer it up"? This meant offering up anything and everything to God, in union with the sufferings of Christ's passion and death on a cross, in an act of atonement for our transgressions. Obviously, one must believe in God, in Jesus Christ and in the Catholic Church's doctrine and teachings on matters such as redemptive suffering, purgatory, heaven and hell, in order to understand, and faithfully follow, these precepts. There is also the basic tenet of the sanctity of life, from the womb to the tomb. There is also end of life care called *Palliative Care*, which is in keeping with the Church's doctrine. The Roman Catholic Diocese of Peterborough offers a comprehensive article on the concept of palliative care on its website, beginning with a definition: "*The*

World Health Organization defines palliative care as "an approach that improves the quality of life of patients and their families facing the problems associated with life-threatening illness, through the prevention and relief of suffering by means of early identification and impeccable assessment and treatment of pain and other problems, physical, psychosocial and spiritual." The intention of palliative care is neither to hasten nor delay death and acknowledges that dying is a normal process."[1] *In addition, The Catechism of the Catholic Church*[2] *(2276) affirms that "those whose lives are diminished or weakened deserve special respect." As such, the Catechism views palliative care as a "special form of disinterested charity [that] should be encouraged" (2279)....Venerable Pope Pius XII was the first Pontiff to justify the use of pain medication in the terminally ill, even if the person's life may be shortened as a result. In Evangelium Vitae, Pope St. John Paul II reiterated: "In such a case (use of painkillers and sedatives), death is not willed or sought, even though for reasonable motives one runs the risk of it: there is simply a desire to ease pain effectively by using the analgesics which medicine provides."*[3] In other words, there are many ways of dealing licitly, compassionately and in keeping with the Church's teachings, with disease, pain, suffering, end-of-life and death without resorting to the legalized killing of vulnerable persons.

---

[1] https://www.peterboroughdiocese.org/en/life-and-faith/palliative-care.aspx

[2] https://www.vatican.va/archive/ENG0015/_INDEX.HTM

[3] https://www.peterboroughdiocese.org/en/life-and-faith/palliative-care.aspx

To begin with, in Canada, there is a legal process in place, across the country, to "help" people end their lives with medical assistance: MAID (Medical Assistance in Dying). The government of Canada has an entire website dedicated to this program: *"Medical assistance in dying (MAID) is a process that allows someone who is found eligible to be able to receive assistance from a medical practitioner in ending their life....a physician or nurse practitioner directly administers a substance that causes death, such as an injection of a drug....a physician or nurse practitioner provides or prescribes a drug that the eligible person takes themselves, in order to bring about their own death...."*[4] There are a few guidelines and stipulations in place to ensure that only in extreme instances will this "assistance" be granted. This being said, as is oftentimes the case for many rules and regulations, abuses and exaggerations do take place, to the point where this type of recourse has become commonplace. Since its inception and legalization, there are more and more Canadians who have been opting for assistance in ending their lives. According to statisca.com, there has been a major increase in the amount of MAID deaths: *"In 2022, there were 13,241 medically assisted deaths in Canada. The number of medically assisted deaths in Canada has increased over the past few years, with only 5,665 such deaths in the year 2019. In 2022, Quebec was the province with the highest number of medically assisted deaths, followed by Ontario and British Columbia. Most medically assisted deaths in Canada are among the elderly, and in most

---

[4] https://www.canada.ca/en/health-canada/services/health-services-benefits/medical-assistance-dying.html

Chapter Eleven: On Euthanasia and Assisted Suicide

cases, natural death is reasonably foreseeable."[5] In fact, there was such an increase in MAID's, that Canada has now surpassed any other country in this regard: *"Quebec passes Netherlands to lead world in number per capita...Quebec is now the jurisdiction with the highest proportion of people choosing medical assistance in dying (MAID), said Michel Bureau, president of the province's Commission on End of Life Care...In Quebec 5.1% of deaths result from MAID,"* he told a press conference. *"In the Netherlands it's 4.8% of deaths and in Belgium 2.3%."...Rates have also been steadily rising in the rest of Canada, reaching 3.3% of all deaths in 2021. Quebec operates under its own MAID law, passed in June 2016."*[6] Furthermore, *"In 2022, there were 13,241 MAID provisions in Canada, bringing the total number of medically assisted deaths in Canada since 2016 to 44,958. In 2022, the total number of MAID provisions increased by 31.2% (2022 over 2021) compared to 32.6% (2021 over 2020). The annual growth rate in MAID provisions has been steady over the past six years, with an average growth rate of 31.1% from 2019 to 2022."*[7] In fact, some people are beginning to raise the alarm about the explosion of medically assisted deaths in Canada. The Canadian Broadcasting Corporation (CBC), via their CBC News website, has reported the following: *"Experts and advocates who spoke with CBC News questioned whether the MAID growth rate and the percentage*

---

[5] https://www.statista.com/statistics/1189552/medically-assisted-death-recipients-nature-of-suffering-canada/#:

[6] https://www.bmj.com/content/379/bmj.o3023

[7] https://www.canada.ca/en/health-canada/services/publications/health-system-services/annual-report-medical-assistance-dying-2022.html

of deaths should be causes for concern... Rebecca Vachon, the program director for health at the non-partisan Christian think tank Cardus,[8] described the year-over-year MAID growth as "alarming."[9] Medical professionals are also adding their voices to this concern. The Toronto Star has also reported that: *"The number of Canadians ending their lives through medically assisted death has grown at a speed that outpaces every other nation in the world....Dr. Sonu Gaind, head of the psychiatry department at Sunnybrook Hospital, said he is concerned about what the surge in medically assisted deaths 'says about our society'."*[10] Indeed, what is this surge reflecting? As far as I can surmise, it reflects the mindset of refusing to take care of our elders. It is much more convenient and cost effective to simply end an ailing, elderly person's life, than to care for them over a more or less lengthy period. It is quite an upheaval in one's life to put everything on hold and, for example, care for one's old and sick mother, sometimes for many years. It demands a great deal of sacrificial love. But didn't this mother sacrifice her own life to care for her children? The prevailing philosophy is to be self-absorbed and only think about one's own happiness and desires. Lingering, ailing, aging parents are not conducive to living one's life as one pleases. Much better to follow the oftentimes quoted "compassionate end" and be done with it; they're old and suffering anyway. How very

---

[8] https://www.cardus.ca/about/our-mission/
[9] https://www.cbc.ca/news/politics/maid-canada-report-2022-1.7009704
[10] https://www.thestar.com/news/investigations/surge-in-medically-assisted-deaths-under-canada-s-maid-program-outpaces-every-other-country/article

Chapter Eleven: On Euthanasia and Assisted Suicide

heartless!! Have people forgotten what our elders have done for us? They paved the way for us, took care of us, sacrificed for us, and this is how they are treated?! As for the old and suffering patients, they feel compelled to get out of the way, not wanting to be a burden on others. How come they feel this way? Perhaps they are made to feel this way, by their very own "loved ones"; that they are indeed a burden to their children and grandchildren because of the implicit reproach that if they were not around, life would be better. As Human Life International,[11] a pro-life organization which I will be discussing further on, eloquently states: *"Caring for loved ones means that we must never allow them to believe they are burdens. Caring for them means we must see the face of Christ in them. It means we must see them through Christ's eyes and reflect Christ's love."*[12] We should all be aware of the perils of selfishness and lack of love towards others; what goes around usually comes around.

With regards to the preponderance of euthanasia and assisted deaths, these legitimate concerns are not exclusive to Canada; Americans are taking note of what is happening to their northern neighbor. They are also voicing concern on the upward spiral of wholesale euthanasia in Canada. The Washington Examiner has written an in-depth report on this issue, stating, among other things, that: *"This would be a cause for great concern on its own. But it is compounded by the reporting done by people such as Alexander Raikin, whose alarming piece exposed*[13] *just how the MAID program takes advantage of*

---

[11] https://www.hli.org/
[12] https://www.hli.org/resources/bible-verses-about-euthanasia/
[13] https://www.thenewatlantis.com/publications/no-other-options

those in poverty. Other reporting[14] *revealed that Canadian doctors are bringing up assisted suicide before their patients do. There seems to be an eagerness to those promoting MAID. Raikin spoke with a doctor who performed more than 300 assisted suicides and said she believes "that the act of offering the option of an assisted death is one of the most therapeutic things we do." A three-minute commercial*[15] *titled "All is Beauty," — which started with a caption reading "the most beautiful exit" — glorified assisted suicide. It later turned out that the woman featured in it, who was euthanized just a few days later, did not actually want to die but felt like she had no other choice."*[16] These types of "advertising" for euthanasia is part of the social trend of using language as an influencing tool, to advance the euthanasia agenda, by brainwashing society into believing that euthanasia is good and desirable. Verbal engineering and social engineering is exactly what is happening for every other social concept being currently advocated: transgenderism, LGBTQ issues, abortion, feminism, contraception and sexual liberty. Ruth Marker, executive director of the International Anti-Euthanasia Task Force[17] and author of *Deadly Compassion* (Wm. Morrow & Co.), once said that "*All social engineering is preceded by verbal engineering*".[18] In 1996, she

---

[14] https://nationalpost.com/news/canada/canada-maid-medical-aid-in-dying-consent-doctors

[15] https://nationalpost.com/news/canada/woman-euthanasia-commercial-wanted-to-live

[16] https://www.washingtonexaminer.com/opinion/2585777/canadas-disturbing-assisted-suicide-experiment-is-going-to-get-much-worse/

[17] https://uia.org/s/or/en/1100054795

[18] https://faithandreason.com/episodes/do-you-hate-me/

Chapter Eleven: On Euthanasia and Assisted Suicide

wrote a comprehensive article entitled "The Art of Verbal Engineering"[19] with Wesley J. Smith, for the Duquesne Law Review, on the subject of euthanasia and assisted dying. What was once regarded as unacceptable has slowly, but surely, become admissible, in large part due to the softening of language, the redefinition of certain words and a major dose of euphemisms. In other words, the language has been engineered towards a new social construct which accepts the killing of our fellow human beings in the name of compassion and rejects the notion of God deciding when our time on earth is over.

There are many cases worldwide of abuses being committed in the name of assisted dying. One case in point is Tom Mortier's fight against the Belgian system of euthanasia. His sixty-four-year-old mother was suffering from depression. He had the shock of his life when he went to the hospital for his regular visit with her and was informed that she had been euthanized. Alliance Defending Freedom International (ADF)[20] took on Mortier's case: *"STRASBOURG (4 October 2022) – In a major case on the right to life, the European Court of Human Rights ruled in favor of Tom Mortier, son of Godelieva de Troyer, who died by lethal injection in 2012, aged 64. Her euthanasia was conducted on the basis of a diagnosis of "incurable depression". In the case of Mortier v. Belgium, the Court found that Belgium violated the European Convention on Human Rights when it failed to properly examine the alarming circumstances leading to her euthanasia.*

---

[19] https://dsc.duq.edu/cgi/viewcontent.cgi?article=3087&context=dlr
[20] https://adfinternational.org/about-us/

The Court held that there was a violation of Article 2 of the European Convention on Human Rights that everyone's right to life shall be protected by law. This judgment was with regard to the way in which the facts surrounding de Troyer's euthanasia were handled by Belgium's Federal Commission for the Control and Evaluation of Euthanasia..."[21] While Tom Mortier won his case, he will never get his mother back.

The spread of euthanasia remains a troubling reality across the world. Human Life International[22] is a pro-life organization that is working to build a society where every life is sacred. They also maintain a website dedicated to the opposing legalized killing, based on the teaching of the Catholic Church: "*...regardless of what the secular world calls it, taking the life of an innocent person—sick, elderly, disabled, or otherwise—is both wrong and immoral. We know this because the Catechism of the Catholic Church teaches that "whatever its motives and means, direct euthanasia consists in putting an end to the lives of handicapped, sick, or dying persons. It is morally unacceptable." It further teaches that "those whose lives are diminished or weakened deserve special respect" (2277).*[23] It is important for everyone to educate and inform themselves on this particular issue, given that no one can escape death; it will happen, sooner or later, in one form or another. We must safeguard the dignity of all human life and not give in to being a mere commodity to be disposed of at

---

[21] https://adfinternational.org/news/tom-mortier-ruling
[22] https://www.hli.org/
[23] https://www.hli.org/resources/bible-verses-about-euthanasia/

the whim of a society which judges that our life is no longer worth living. God is the ultimate decision-maker; not us.

Conclusion

Sunday evening. Final days of summer.

Here I am, sitting in front of my little computer. What started as a project of putting my thoughts to paper has culminated in eleven chapters devoted to the burning questions of our times. Everyone seems to be taking sides on issues of personal freedom, which affects all of humanity. The personal choices we make affect society, be it sexual orientation, contraception and abortion, marriage and children, living and dying, sexual freedom, and on and on…Everybody is protesting for one right or another, all over the globe. Society has changed dramatically in the past sixty years, not necessarily for the better, in many respects.

Frankly, I believe that a return to traditional values and religious values might help to stem the tide of self-destruction that seems to be humanity's path at this time in history. The current ideological landscape and culture of lesbian/gay/homosexual/transgender/contraception/abortion/sexual-freedom-without-children/adultery/euthanasia/atheism does not lead to procreation, hence the path towards self-extinction.

I believe that it all comes down to a very simple observation, which was voiced by one of the deacons in my parish, at this morning's Sunday Mass: Who will you choose to follow? Society or God?

As far as I can tell, society is rejecting God and wants to construct its own subjective reality. I, for one, want to live in objective reality, based on biological truth and Divine Revelation. Ergo, I choose to follow God.

www.ingramcontent.com/pod-product-compliance
Lightning Source LLC
LaVergne TN
LVHW051834080426
835512LV00018B/2864